Stalked!

My Encounter with a Colorado Bigfoot

• FOR •

Mindy

Introduction

by Rusty Wilson

If you've read any of my Bigfoot Campfire Stories, you'll know that I meet many interesting and sometimes unusual characters as a fly-fishing guide. One of these was Brad Morris, and even though he didn't want to tell his story around the campfire, he did agree to tell it to me in private.

And I was glad he did, for it's one of the more unusual and gripping stories I've heard, and I've heard quite a number. Brad's story has a certain level of poignancy mixed with terror, something that you'll just have to read to really get. And what a story it is!

As I write this, I'm reminded of a very excited email I received from a friend who had just spent two weeks alone backpacking in the same region in which Brad had his Bigfoot encounter. My friend is a landscape photographer who spends much of his time alone in the wilds all over the world. We've discussed Bigfoot many times, and he refused to grant it any credence. After all, he'd been in some of the planet's wildest places and never seen any indication that Bigfoot might exist.

That was true until he came across a set of footprints off-trail far in the wilds of Colorado's San Juan Mountains. He said it gave him a really strange feeling, and he felt like he was being watched. Those prints were found very near Brad's encounter.

After hearing Brad's account and seeing the photos my photographer friend sent me, I'm convinced that Bigfoot is alive and well in Colorado's rugged mountains. I hope I'm right, and if so, I wish the creatures well. We need to keep the wild alive in all its variations, and it's stories like Brad's that remind us of our place in the grand scheme of things.

May Bigfoot flourish, and I hope you enjoy Brad's story as much as I did.

—Rusty Wilson

PREFACE

I know many people don't believe in Bigfoot, and let me say right up front that I myself was once one of these. I used to think that by now there should be ample proof of Bigfoot's existence, considering how we humans have now set our footprints nearly everywhere on the planet. Bigfoot should definitely be in museums by now, was my line of reasoning, and we should have many catalogued bones and maybe even have captured one alive, as we have with nearly every other species on the planet.

But when I looked into it, I discovered that we really haven't captured nor catalogued every species on the planet, not by a long shot. Some biologists estimate that there are about 9 million species on the Earth, and we have only catalogued maybe 2 million. This means that nearly 80% of all species on Earth remain undiscovered.

But even though I didn't believe in Bigfoot, I actually had every reason to. But I was in deep denial, having sublimated and forgotten my memories, as you will soon see.

I hope my story helps some of you to gain some insight into the depths of what is left of our wilderness—the pristine origins of our ancient ancestors. Not only the real wilderness outside of our selves, but perhaps more importantly, the wilderness that still lies in the depths of our individual hearts.

After all, our civilization is really only a relatively recent phenomenon, covering over our instinctual selves—those selves that evolved primarily in the wilderness.

It has really been a burden for me to keep this all pent up for nearly thirty years now—since 1986, a whole generation gone by. I now have grandchildren who won't ever understand the naive world I was living in then (there wasn't even an Internet yet). Everything has changed enormously since back then.

My twenty-something daughter finally suggested that I try to tell my story and share it as it is, so I can maybe put it all to rest, or at least relieve some of the trauma. She was the first person to ever hear all of it at once.

I agreed with her that I should try to get it all out and off of my chest. So here it is, my story.

ONE: FACING THE DARKNESS

The chilly wind caused the dark Blue Spruce, Engelmann, and Ponderosa pines to sigh in their shadows. The stars seemed to sway above like little Chinese lanterns in the sky, twinkling and glittering in the crystal-clear, cloudless atmosphere. I love the night sky in Colorado.

The wind would start way up above on Green Mountain, and you could hear it up there, like a huge sighing giant blowing his huge lungs out across the trees. It would then grow louder and louder, as it traveled down the mountain, until it was here, blowing my hair about my face and making it downright chilly for a few minutes. The wind would then die out again, and the temperature would get a little warmer in the tall dewy grasses that lined the sandy mountain trails.

A vast dark plain stretched out to the black horizon to the east, a distant prairie peppered with bright flashes of white lightning that would momentarily light up the red, black and brown clouds from which they arced.

The shockingly bright lights of cities lit up the darkness in the closer foreground, with stop lights turning green, yellow, then red once more. There was no traffic there, just a synchrony of uselessness at this hour—3 a.m.

The view here was immense, as the Earth joined the vast starry sky, with the Milky Way splattered across the expanse of the zenith, a vastness of matter and space unimaginably huge.

I sat in the southern shadow of one of the huge Flatirons up above the city of Boulder, Colorado, a four-hundred-foot tall wedge of sandstone that jutted almost straight up behind me into the dark sky, blocking the view to the north.

It was August, 1986.

I remember that it was a glorious night, and the stars were twinkling a brilliant blue white, with Mars glowing red in the east, Jupiter a white dot in the constellation Gemini. I felt like I could see forever up there—I was nearly 2,000 feet vertical above Denver (thirty five miles away) and the perspective—looking down on everything as if it were only a toy—was helping me to feel better about what had happened a couple of weeks ago.

The occurrences then had changed me forever, and it would be some time before I could sleep a full night without waking up in terror, on edge from the trauma. I had to come out here, in what was left of the wilds above the city, in the dark, in spite of all that had happened, so that I might put some of my fears to rest.

I am even now compelled to seek out the wilderness, but now I finally know why. It was a mystery to me for years, but it's now clear.

I had to learn to forgive my father, who had died just three years earlier, killed in a freak accident. He was a lineman, and a telephone pole they were lifting to set into the ground slipped out of the cradle it was in and fell on him, killing him instantly. He was only 52 when he died, and I hadn't spoken to him in over two years, due to a rift we had that I will always feel guilty about, with no way to make it right.

I shivered a little from the chill wind and pulled the hood of my rain parka closer around my face. I wasn't so cold that I would need a winter parka, so I had brought only my rain jacket for protection from the wind and the chill that comes along at this altitude at this time of night, even in the summer.

I had my daypack—the same daypack I was wearing when it all happened—with water and a couple of granola bars in it, plus extra batteries for my flashlight, some matches to build an emergency fire, my monocular—stuff like that. I thought to myself that the pack probably still had dirt and sand from the mountains in it—scant evidence of what had so recently happened.

I realized then that it wasn't just the wind that was making me shiver—I was still scared. After all, it had only been twelve days.

I wasn't a psychologist, so I didn't really know if this was good therapy or not, especially so soon after it all. But eventually, I decided that I'd had enough of this type of treatment, so I clicked my little metal flashlight back on, preparing to walk down the sandy trail back to my car, a mile and a half away. I had accomplished what I had set out to do—go into the wilds again—although some would argue that Chautauqua Park really isn't in the wilds, being so close to downtown Boulder.

TWO: RIDING THE RAILS

I had first seen the Bigfoot three weeks earlier, when finally I got away to Durango—on Colorado's Western Slope, some 350 miles from Boulder—for my annual paid vacation. I was a computer programmer back then in Boulder, working for a company whose name everyone would recognize.

I had to get out and away from the tediousness of my work once in a while and into the wilderness, where I found my only solace in a world of what was usually high-speed frustration, futile tail-chasing, and often brainless tedium. Although I lived in the city, I was not really built for the mindless maze of endless traffic, the scampering for survival, the furious Rat Race. I was drawn instead to the woods.

So, I saw a Bigfoot—and yes, I said Bigfoot. I know many don't believe in Bigfoot, and neither did I until less than a month ago, when I came to believe in a big way. Now, I not only believe in Bigfoot, but I scoff at those who are lucky enough not to know, but act as if they do. But I am getting ahead of myself, so I'll start at the beginning.

I'd always wanted to climb the Fourteeners in southwestern Colorado. Fourteeners are mountain peaks that rise more than fourteen thousand feet above sea level. There are 52 or 54 peaks in Colorado that fit this category—depending on who you talk to and their methods of measurement. The difference is due to prominence, aka "relief"—the amount of mountain that juts up from base to top, without taking sea level into account. In other words, the peaks are all above fourteen thousand feet, but some of them are right next to each other, with small saddles between them.

The mountain with the most prominence in Colorado is Pigeon Peak—just a couple of miles from the Fourteeners in the Needle Mountains—where this story occurs, in the southwestern part of the state. The prominence of Pigeon is 6,000 feet or so, rising up in only two and a half miles from the Animas River, giving some idea as to how steep these mountains are—extremely steep!

I have managed to climb 13 of Colorado's Fourteeners, some along the Front Range, some in the Collegiate Range, and some in the San Juan Range. I stopped climbing mountains only a couple of years after all of this occurred. I found I had lost the passion for it, and not in small part because of what happened. I am now just too anxious for it to be enjoyable.

The Weiminuche Wilderness is about 500,000 acres set aside in the southwestern corner of Colorado, in the San Juan Mountains. The Continental Divide cuts in a northwest-southeast line, zigzagging across the Wilderness. The average elevation in the Weiminuche Wilderness is over 10,000 feet above sea level.

My Dad had always "threatened" to take me out to an area of the Weiminuche called Chicago Basin, where he had hiked when he was a young man, long before I was born, and he had always said he wanted to show it to me.

Unfortunately, we never got to go together, so I was thinking about him the whole trip.

The Weiminuche, south and southeast of Silverton, has three of Colorado's Fourteeners in it—Sunlight, Windom, and Eolus, with North Eolus a sub-peak of Eolus that some consider a separate mountain (although it is only 159 vertical feet difference from Eolus proper, so others don't consider it a separate peak. Prominence, you know).

Anyway, I could maybe climb three—or four—more Fourteeners in my three-week backpacking trip that I had meticulously planned over the course of the year. I was stoked.

The previous year, I had climbed Mt. Elbert—Colorado's highest at 14,440 feet above sea level, and only 65 feet shorter than Mt. Whitney in California, the highest mountain in the contiguous 48 States. I had also summited Mt. Massive (second highest in Colorado) and I made an attempt on La Plata Peak, but lightning and hail ran me out.

I was only out for a week that trip, as the peaks above Leadville (the Collegiate Range, with many peaks named for famous U.S. colleges) are much closer to where I live, and it requires a lot less time and energy to get to them.

The trek to the 14,000-foot peaks in the Weiminuche Wilderness above Silverton requires either a two-mile slog down Molas Pass—with eighty pounds of camping gear on one's back—where there is a bridge to cross the river, then up the Animas River canyon for seven miles, oftentimes on the railroad tracks, hoping not to see a train coming—there are places where you might either get hit by the train or have to jump off a cliff into the raging river.

Then a long climb into Chicago Basin (where the three—or four—Fourteeners loom above), another seven or eight miles, an arduous total of seventeen miles—a rough trip for even the hardy, and I have never been one of those.

Or you can ride the Durango and Silverton Narrow Gauge Railroad from Durango and get let out at the base of the Chicago Basin trail at Needleton, leaving only the seven steep miles, up the Needle Creek Trail, to get up to base camp in Chicago Basin—enough exertion for even the steadfast.

I opted for the latter. I figured that, in addition to the mileage I wouldn't have to walk, riding the train itself would also be a hoot. (Note: you have to schedule the right train ahead of time, as they don't all stop to let off hikers).

But riding the train turned out to be not such a hoot, after all. The coal-fired engine puts out a continuous stream of fine ash that gets painfully into your eyes, making it hard to see. If you ever do ride that train, be sure to wear protective goggles that won't allow the ash into your eyes. It is like getting fine-grit sand in your eyes—not very pleasant.

Anyway, I finally made it to the trailhead, after having driven all night to get to Durango, then catching the train the next morning at 8:00 A.M. It was now 11:00, and I was already pretty bushed.

But I still had to lug my eighty pounds of gear up the seven miles of steep trail. I would sleep really, really well tonight, I supposed.

I usually like to climb and hike alone, because you invariably find that if you are with someone else, you always end up in conversation, which alerts the wildlife in the area of your presence, scaring it away. I like to view and photograph wildlife, and even when I am with someone who also enjoys it, we always end up talking, usually losing a rare opportunity.

Along with this, I am a little antisocial, and I like to get out where I can be alone sometimes. I am of Scottish descent, and I guess I am just another Dour Scot, who prefers that everybody just leave me the hell alone sometimes.

When I was getting ready to get off of the train, several tourists who had been asking me where I was going wished me well. One nice lady asked me with concern, "What are you going to do about all of the animals out there?" A man in a colorful Hawaiian shirt and golfing shorts even said, "Three weeks in the Wilderness? I approve!"

I chuckle at the memory, because for some reason he reminded me of Clark Kent, Superman's alter ego. I guess it was the retro black horn-rimmed glasses he was wearing. Plus, he was very buff, as if he were a weight lifter. I told them not to worry—I had done this before—and I thanked them for their concern as I prepared to get off of the train.

THREE: THE BONE

I now clambered down off of the train, my backpack and water bottles an unruly load in my hands that I now had to get down to the ground, then onto my back somehow. It all suddenly felt really heavy, and I groaned inwardly. "This is going to kick my butt," I thought to myself. Even though I'd been working out more the last couple of months, it probably hadn't been enough.

I managed to get the damned thing onto my back, and I awkwardly strode up the rugged trail, trying to get my "sea legs," as the tourists still on the train took my picture, wishing me well. I waved and walked on up the trail. My little camp pan I used for making coffee clanked behind me, keeping time to the rhythm of my gait.

I crossed a wooden trestle footbridge over the roaring Animas River. It swayed on its cables, spooking me a little. Then I paralleled the river for a while, the trail gradually climbing above the level of the train stretched out on the tracks on the other side of the river—a long yellow and black assemblage of machinery and tourists, who leaned out of the windows to get better views, snapping photographs.

Cameras were in every window, and I suddenly felt what it might be like to be famous, if only for a couple of minutes. The engineer opened a safety valve on the locomotive, and it suddenly chuffed loudly as it sent a cloud of steam billowing from under the main boiler. The sound echoed far above me.

The river was near bank-full, and it was full of roaring white rapids. The sound it made was soothing, yet it somehow also added to my anticipation. I had made it—at least this far—and I was now exhilarating in the luxurious wilderness.

The canyon was lush and green, and full of tall Ponderosas and Blue Spruce trees. The canyon walls climbed steeply up to giant foothills that abutted even larger granite peaks, their flanks being the only part visible, as the higher peaks were blocked by the angles of the forested slopes lower down.

"I wish Dad were here to see this right now," I thought. "This is awesome!"

I was about four hundred yards up a gentle hillside when the train's engineer blew the whistle. It was amazingly loud, making me jump, as I was not expecting it. It could be heard echoing way up into the tall pines, where I imagined giant cliffs of granite and quartzite stood below the final heights of the Fourteeners soaring high and bleak above them, reflecting the sound seconds later and giving me a sonic sense of the majestic open spaces yet to come.

These were the Needle Mountains, and they are without a doubt the most magnificent and isolated high peaks in Colorado—maybe in the entire coterminous United

States. I was now down in the Animas River canyon, however, and I could not yet see any of the peaks—I could just hear the echoes of the whistle that bounced back down, and they lasted a long time before they finally died out. The roar of the river breathed underneath it all, a continuous winsome sigh.

After only a few minutes I was already getting winded, climbing and toiling uphill, so I stopped for a few minutes to acclimate, sitting on a big rock and watching the train as it clanked and groaned, slowly accelerating up the Animas River canyon. Black smoke surged out of the smokestack, and I felt a little sorry for those still on board who had to get that crap in their eyes. The D&SNG Railroad really should warn people to wear proper protective eyewear.

The engineer gave two more farewell blasts on the whistle, and the long reverberating decay of the echoes from up above died out finally, giving way once again to the roar of the Animas. I oddly wondered what the echoes would look like to a bat. I listened to the train for a few minutes as it chuffed and clanked up the canyon, eventually getting too far away to hear over the roaring of the river.

I turned and started walking again. It was already nearly 11:30, and I would have to keep going at a pretty good pace if I were to get to Chicago Basin before twilight. The sun went down in the high basins in the San Juan Mountains a little earlier than out in the open horizon, as the nearby peaks, aretes, passes, and glacial cirques all conspire to create tall shadows, causing an early sunset up here. Also, after the sun sets here, it starts to get pretty cold—even in the summer—and you really should be ready to put on some clothes and hunker down for the evening, because it only gets colder until morning, when the warm sun finally crests over the tall, jagged eastern horizon.

A few years ago up in Vestal Basin, a few miles away as the crow flies from where I was now, it registered a nippy twenty-five degrees above zero on the little thermometer I carry in my survival kit. It was really cold that night, in spite of my state-of-the-art mountain gear. My washcloth had frozen stiff, hanging over one of my tent tensioning lines. It took me a few cups of hot tea to finally get myself warm that morning.

Incidentally, you are not allowed to light an open fire in this wilderness, because too many people trash the forest, building more and more fire rings until they are every-where. Backpacking stoves are the only option left for heating food, coffee, or tea—if you want to be cool and help the wilderness stay wild, that is.

Since I try to keep my pack weight down as much as possible, I carry a summer sleeping bag—instead of a three- or four-season bag—and just put on extra clothes when it gets too cold. That time in Vestal Basin, I had everything on, and I was still shivering as I made hot tea that morning. As I said, this was only a few miles north of where I was now.

I now struggled with my breathing and I had a hard time getting into a good rhythm. I climbed up a steep set of switchbacks above the river, then up a gentler, rounded hill. I was nearly to the top of the little hill when I decided I needed to stop for a few minutes and catch my breath again.

I wasn't used to the altitude yet—it takes a good eight or ten hours to start to acclimate up here, and I would feel much better after having slept at altitude—although it can take up to four days if you have changed altitude very drastically. I was only increasing my usual altitude at home by a about a mile or so—it's not like I was suddenly climbing in the Himalayas, or anything. I would just have to rough it out until I got to a suitable campsite several miles ahead, up the trail.

I stopped near the top of the rounded hillside on the edge of a little gulch and took my bulky pack off, backing up to a big boulder where it was easier to remove. I unzipped the top compartment (where I keep the gear I might need on the trail), pulling out a sandwich I had packed that morning.

When I pulled the sandwich out, my survival kit—packed into a blaze orange waterproof bag—caught on the edge of the brown paper bag, popping out of the pack's top compartment and rolling off of the boulder. It bounced down into the gulch about twenty five or thirty feet, jumping up over a couple of logs below me and finally coming to rest under a bunch of ferns, in a little hollow where the slope was flatter. I had carefully watched where it went, so I could find it easily (this wasn't the first time I had ever dropped something).

I put the sandwich down and carefully walked down the gentle slope, wet with the dew in the lush vegetation that grew in the shadows. My boots glistened with water and my lower legs got immediately wet.

I ducked under several tree branches, climbing awkwardly up over the mossy logs to the little hollow where I could see the bright orange color of the survival kit contrasting sharply with the dim shadows and dark green undergrowth.

When I bent down to get the kit, I noticed an odd patch of white and red in the soil under a fern, in the center of a ring of tall trees, whose hidden roots made the ground really uneven and difficult to balance on. The glowing white contrasted sharply with the gloom there under the fern, catching my eye.

I retrieved my survival kit, then I bent down and pulled the whitish piece out of the ground, thinking it might be an oddly shaped rock—but I immediately knew it was no rock, as it had the characteristic raspy, splintery texture of bone.

I pulled it up out of the dark, matted pine needles and rich loamy soil, and I realized that I was now holding a portion of a backbone—a large vertebra, with long 'wings', or apophyses, reminding me of cow skeletons I have seen in the desert in Utah.

The bone was packed with dirt and detritus, so I cleaned it off, wiping the soil away with my hand. It was really red, and I thought at first it might still have blood on it. But I looked closer, and it was just the iron oxide in the soil, having stained the once white bone a bright red in places.

I could now see more patches of white sticking out of the dark soil, where I had disturbed it. I recognized a rib and several more vertebrae, but I decided one bone was enough, considering how much I already had to carry. It seemed weird to find a buried carcass out here. It was under several feet of dirt, and the only reason I had even noticed it was because I had to bend over a fallen log to get to my survival pack.

I had apparently found the burial site of some large animal, and I decided I would have my friend Jeremy have a look at the bone, back in Boulder. He was going to college there, studying paleontology and comparative anatomy, and I knew he would have fun trying to determine what kind of critter the bone was from. I figured it must be a bear or something, based on its size. It seemed that it might be really old, buried under that much dirt.

I carried it gingerly in my right hand, not really wanting to touch it much, having a natural aversion to such things. I held the survival pack tightly in my left hand, as I didn't really want to drop it again.

After stepping over a long fallen tree, I lost my balance and came down on one knee. Fortunately, I was able to grab onto a small sapling, dropping the bone but keeping myself from being injured too badly.

I cut my right knee on a rock, but it was only a small gash, and it stopped bleeding after I held my handkerchief on it for a couple of minutes. If I had been wearing pants instead of shorts, I might not have cut it at all. I picked up the bone again, after searching under some leaves for it, and then continued climbing.

When I got back up to my backpack, I carefully wrapped the bone in an old t-shirt, burying it in what seemed like a secure place, down in some clothing where it wouldn't break inside my big backpack. After drinking some water, I hoisted the heavy pack once again up onto my shoulders.

As I did so, I suddenly got the feeling that somebody was watching me from the gloominess of the shadows in the forest across the little gulch. I stopped and looked into the shadows there intently, but I saw nothing, finally shrugging it off as simply paranoia from being alone in the wilderness. Finding strange bones in the gloom was creeping me out a little, I guessed.

I hiked on up the trail to the top of the little hill. The trail now crossed a series of meadows and flatter shelves along the upper drainage edge. I felt better, and my breathing finally settled into a good strong rhythm, giving me more energy.

I was just starting to get into a good second wind when I thought I saw something bright glint in the corner of my vision, there in the shadows of the deep woods just below me. I stopped for a few seconds, and held my breath, as I had been panting pretty loud.

Everything was deathly still, and I wondered why the birds weren't out singing. I should have taken this as an immediate warning signal of some sort, but I was too caught up in the moment, so I ignored it. The only sound was the river, roaring way down below me now. I now felt odd, like the world had stopped spinning for a few seconds.

The sweat was dripping from my forehead, getting into my glasses and annoying me, so I decided to take off my backpack to dig through it and get out a bandanna to tie around my forehead to sop up the sweat.

I walked about twenty yards further, where a big Ponderosa pine trunk stood by the trail, about three feet tall where it had been chain-sawed off by the Forest Service. It was just the right height to be of use in taking my pack off and putting it back on. I backed up and parked the pack on the stump, wriggling out of the straps again.

Once off, I balanced the pack against a nearby smaller tree, and unzipped the top pocket where—like I said—I keep my immediate trail needs, like sunscreen, mosquito dope, lip balm, a bandanna, etc.

I pulled out the bandanna and started to tie it around my forehead. It was still deathly quiet, and I started to feel uneasy again for some reason, like I was being watched. Flies weren't even buzzing around, like they usually did. I held my breath again, and listened intently, holding very still.

Nothing. Absolutely nothing made any sound, and I was amazed at how quiet it was up here. I listened closely for a couple of minutes, but I still heard nothing—just the river, far below now, roaring way off like a sigh in the distance.

Still, I felt like something was watching me—the hackles were up on my neck. I looked around keenly, intently searching for the source of the weird feeling, looking down into the dark trees below, looking at the dark trees on the slopes above, looking down the trail I had come from. Nothing. I thought of the bone again, wrapped in the t-shirt and securely buried in my pack. Was I somehow violating some sacred precept by taking it? Or was I just being paranoid again?

I tried to shrug the weird feeling off as just a nearby elk or something, watching me. But I realized that elk had way keener senses than to let a human chance accidentally upon them, and they probably don't make a habit of observing people for recreation. It might have been a bear, but I think they are more wary of us than we are of them, especially considering we are the ones who usually have the guns.

Speaking of guns, I don't carry one when I am backpacking, because I don't feel they are really necessary. A big gun just weighs too much—bullets and all—and a small gun wouldn't do the trick, especially if you are being attacked by a bear. Besides, I believe you have to have a concealed carry permit to have a gun in your backpack.

I do carry a big can of bear spray, however, and I now thought about digging it out. But I decided that I was just being paranoid, it being the first time I had been out alone for quite a while, so I left the bear spray buried deep in the pack.

I am hesitant to say it, but I also used to carry M80s back then, although they were illegal. (For those who may not know, an M80 is an explosive charge, about the size of an eighth of a stick of dynamite, with a fast fuse. You have to throw it in a hurry, or it will explode in your hand, potentially blowing off a finger or two).

I figured that, as a last line of defense, an M80 would scare the daylights out of a bear—if I could get it lit in time. I carried one of them in my shirt pocket, and I had a Zippo lighter in my pants pocket, so everything was handy.

I got the M80s from a farmer friend of my Dad's, who used them to blow little detritus dams out of his irrigation ditches. The M80s didn't weigh much—I only carried four or five of them—and I didn't think I would ever use them anyway. I definitely never used them for recreation or pranks.

I drank another big swig of water from one of the gallon jugs that I carry with me—one in each hand as I hike, and four tied to my backpack. Like I said, my pack ends up weighing about eighty pounds when I finally have it all together. About 30 pounds of this is water weight, plus I carry eight pounds of water in each hand.

I also carry iodine for water purification, in case I end up in a situation without any fresh drinking water. I have had Giardiasis before—caused by bacteria in unpurified drinking water—and believe me, it's no picnic. I was sick off and on for six weeks before I finally went to the clinic and got antibiotics.

I now grabbed a few mouthfuls of trail mix, replacing the bag back into the backpack. I then checked all of my lashings, tightening them as I went. A heavy pack is easier to carry if it is tight, as it won't sway as much.

The breeze picked up a bit, and the excellent scent of real pine blew into my nostrils, along with the smell of bluebells and columbines. There were entire mountainsides of them up here, along with fireweed and skunk cabbage.

It was beautiful up here, but I had a strange sense of foreboding, and I knew that any little misstep I made could lead to disaster. The wilderness is a two-edged sword: a place of sublime beauty, but also a place of wild extremes, and even sudden death.

With this dire thought in my mind, I checked my map to see approximately where I was. I recognized the hillside up above me, comparing it to the contours on the topo (topographical map). I was only about two and a half miles above Needleton now. I still had a long walk ahead of me—about five or six steep miles, with all of that horrible weight on my back. But I sensed the agony would be worth it, and I suddenly felt inspired again.

I backed up against the heavy backpack on the tree stump, pulling it to me and chucking it back onto my shoulders, yanking the straps forward roughly to tighten them. I stood up with effort, snapped the plastic buckle on the thick lumbar pad around my waist, and walked on for about forty-five more minutes.

I now looked at my watch, hanging on a lanyard tied to my backpack. It was already 1:30 in the afternoon. I might just have to camp below Chicago Basin proper, then hike on up tomorrow, moving my base camp after I had rested. I was feeling more than a little bushed—after all, I had already been awake for over twelve hours now. Time seemed like it was rushing quickly, as the last two hours had seemed like only a few minutes.

Like I said, I had driven from Boulder to Durango—a six and a half-hour trip—and I had only just made it to the train in time at 8:00 this morning. I had only slept about three hours last night (I was anxious to go), and I had been up since 1:00 A.M.—over twelve hours awake already, and the day only half over.

I suddenly felt really weary, and I decided it was time for some lunch. After topping another rise, I found a little spot off of the trail. I managed to get my backpack off again, leaning it against a big Ponderosa Pine trunk, being careful not to get any sap on it.

There was a boulder here, and it made a good seat and lunch table. I pulled out a couple more of the sandwiches I had fixed late yesterday and ate them, washing them down with water. I got up and surveyed the immediate area, striding around and watching for movement in the trees. There was still no sound, and the utter silence seemed surreal.

Suddenly, I felt really exhausted—I was amazed at how tired I now was. It was as if a big weight was pressing down on my chest, and I found it hard to breathe all of a sudden. I tried to fight the sudden feeling of stupor I was having, but it was no use.

I sat down, plopping on the ground next to my pack. I leaned against the big tree, tilted my head back, and looked up into the thick branches with their fragrant boughs of green needles and pinecones. The sun was hot and noticeably past the zenith. I had to keep going or I would never get where I needed to be, but it was no use—I gave in to the grogginess, and I fell fast asleep.

FOUR: BEARS AND BOMBS

I dreamed that I was in a dark cave, way up in the high mountains, up above the tree line. It was cold, so cold. I was looking out past the dark jumbled rocks that lay inside, out of the black mouth of the cave into the cold moonlit landscape that lay outside. It was nighttime, in the wee hours, and it was very cold—in fact, it was the cold that had awakened me.

I was lying down now in a twiggy, grassy nest, curled up tightly in the fetal position. I could see my breath as I exhaled into the backlight coming from the frigid sky outside of the cave. It was really, really cold. I got up, pushing myself up with my hands, resigned to not being able to sleep any more.

I had to get out of there and find a better, warmer shelter somewhere, somehow. Something stank to high heaven, but I barely noticed the stench—as if I had previously grown used to it. It seemed odd that I would notice it at all, considering how cold it was. I shivered, and I realized oddly that shivering was something I never did.

It was so cold, so cold—I thought I was going to die. I was shivering violently now, and the condensation from my lungs hung in the air after I exhaled. I could even see individual tiny icicles form around my breath, like little microscopic spears of pallid light, falling through the air as it wafted through the eerie blue-white moonlight that streamed into the darkness of the cave.

I crept up slowly to the cave entrance. I somehow knew instinctively where every rock and obstacle in the cave was, as if I had been there before. When I got to the entrance, I leaned out to have a look around me, grabbing the edge of the wall where it met with the outer world. My hand was covered in thick, black fur, but I just thought it was a sub-zero glove, and I gave it no mind. It seemed to be of no consequence, really.

I remembered the bone now, and I went back inside the cave to retrieve it. I had wrapped it in a snowshoe hare's hide that I had saved from a hunting trip. It was buried under a big rock, which I now rolled aside in order to get at it. Ah! It was still there, safe. I then returned to the cave's mouth for a look at the landscape, the bone in the hide wrapped snugly under my armpit.

I was now standing at the edge of a circle of rocks piled at the cave's mouth, looking down the dark slope into a huge snow-filled bowl, surrounded by tall, threatening blue-black mountains, with the cold stars glowing and shimmering brightly beyond, in the inky black sky above.

The half-moon cast an eerie pale blue-white light over the vast bowl of snow, with the jagged edges of peaks outlining the night sky beyond. The cave was set into the headwall of one of the bowl's interior slopes, far up on the side of one of the immense icy, ragged mountains—dark frozen teeth, waiting to bite.

The raw wind suddenly blew tiny ice crystals all around me, scattering and glinting weirdly in the moonlight. The blast chilled me further, making me shiver even more.

Far below me, I could just make out the black tree line in the frigid gray darkness, where I knew I would have to go in order to build a fire, at least.

But the idea of "fire" also seemed odd and out of place in my thoughts, as if I only had a vague inkling of what that was. "What is fire?" I thought, and I felt an odd dissonance, and I wondered for a moment what I had become now—who was I? How could I ever get warm again?

I nervously fingered the bone wrapped in the hide, now anxious that it would somehow disappear forever from me.

Far above me, the cold blue-white stars twinkled, but I had a strange, unsettling sense that I could no longer recognize the constellations of my youth. It was so cold—so cold—that it made my eyes hurt to look, and they instantly watered up. I suddenly felt very lost and alone, as if on an alien planet. I was utterly, irrevocably isolated and forsaken.

A strange sadness overcame me, and I called out in anguish, bellowing out at the top of my lungs, screaming to the night sky, with the instant echo of my anguished apprehension reflecting back to me from the jagged teeth of night.

Suddenly, I was awake, and the loose bark of the Ponderosa tree was sticking to the back of my sweating neck. I immediately brushed it off, and then suddenly noticed that the sun had dipped significantly lower in the western sky. I thought I heard something strange echoing far across the valley, but I figured it might be the train again—returning to Durango from Silverton. My neck was sore from sleeping at such an odd angle.

"Dammit! What time is it?" I wondered, disappointed that I could be so careless. I reached around to the watch that hung from my backpack's zipper (I hate wearing a watch on my wrist—I am too obsessive, looking at the time every two minutes and driving myself crazy). I saw that it was already almost four o'clock in the afternoon.

I reached into the big backpack and checked obsessively for the bone. It was still there, wrapped tightly in the t-shirt. I strangely felt relieved when I realized it was safe.

I had slept for nearly two and a half hours! No wonder my neck was sore! I must have been really tired, because normally I wouldn't be able to sleep in this contorted position.

I was really behind schedule now, and I would either have to try to hike on up to my destination using my flashlight in the dark—somewhat dangerous in the rough terrain—or find a lower place to camp. I hated setting up camp in the dark, because it made me feel like I was desperately trying to beat the clock.

I decided to look at the topo map again, to find a lower campsite. I would only have a few hours to get there and get set up before darkness set in. I cursed my stupid luck, as what looked like the nearest decent place was still three and a half miles away, up steep terrain. I repacked everything, put on the pack, and got ready to walk away.

I suddenly heard an unnerving howl that put the hair on my neck up, and I instantly realized that the echo that

I had imagined was the train whistle had been something else entirely.

Whatever had made that noise was very, very large, as the sound seemed to go on forever, rising and lowering in pitch like a wolf howl, only very much deeper and longer, with no breaks to get another breath. It finally stopped after at least a minute, and the sound seemed to carry on forever into the tall peaks, echoing and reverberating as it finally died out, leaving only the silence.

I now felt extremely exposed and vulnerable. "What in the hell was that?" I thought as the goose bumps rose on my arms. My heart immediately started beating much faster, and I blanched, feeling suddenly very weak, exposed, and frightened.

Whatever had made that enormous, gut-wrenching noise was just down the mountain from me, not very far away—maybe only a couple of hundred yards. I peered nervously down into the now lengthening shadows of the tall trees below me, but I didn't see any obvious movement. Was it after the bone—whatever it was? Why would I think that? For some reason I now felt oddly guilty for having taken it.

I stood for a minute, listening intently, with my heart pounding rapidly in my chest. I was afraid to move, thinking I would give myself away.

I felt paralyzed. But I was also on the verge of running away willy-nilly, panicked and terrified through the thick forest all around me. That would not be a good idea, especially with the awkward pack on. I intentionally calmed myself, making myself take deep breaths.

Suddenly something came crashing through the brush, running full tilt abruptly into an aspen grove about a hundred yards below me—a big black lumbering beast, running on all fours—a bear! It was coming up the hill, straight at me!

Had I somehow gotten between it and its cubs? It would be on me in only a few seconds, and I grabbed the M80 instinctively out of my shirt pocket.

I fumbled in my pants pocket for my Zippo, got it lit after a few tries, and set the fuse on the firecracker sputtering. I threw it violently away from me, downhill toward the bear, which was now only about forty yards away, running directly towards me, like it didn't even see me. I hoped I wouldn't start a forest fire, but it was too late to turn back now.

The M80 arced down the hillside leaving a trace of blue smoke from the fuse, then—BOOM!!—it exploded, sending shrapnel of little twigs and leaves splattering all around. The sudden sound was enormous, echoing all around the mountains seemingly forever.

The bear swerved a little to go around the spot where the M80 had exploded, then ran on up the hill, passing me within ten yards and not batting an eye, as if the M80 was something it was used to. I could distinctly hear its labored breathing, making little whining noises as if it were running for its life.

I hadn't scared it nearly as much as whatever it was running from had. The bear now disappeared into a grove of Blue Spruce above me, crashing into the thick underbrush.

I was in shock, and my heartbeat fluttered crazily. I looked closely at the spot in the brush down below where the bear had come from, and I thought I saw something white moving swiftly away, down the hill into the darker shadows. I stood there for what seemed like an eternity, just breathing and watching intently.

I looked around up the hill to where the bear had disappeared, wondering if it would come back. I felt stuck now, like no matter which way I went, I would be in danger. I turned back and forth, looking up, then down the hill for movement. Nothing.

I finally decided after a few minutes that I had to do something—to take action, any action. I turned and walked as quietly and as quickly as I could manage up the trail, consciously placing every footstep in a safe place. I was now scaring myself to death, and I wished I could just walk quieter, so I could hear what was going on around me.

My footfalls seemed deafening now, and the creaking of my backpack was maddening. The little pan clanked gently, even though I was trying to walk so it wouldn't.

What had frightened the bear so much? Was whatever it was still there? And where did the bear go?

I have lived in Colorado all of my life, and only seen a handful of bears—none of them up close and personal, though. And none of them had been running towards me in a panic.

I stopped every couple of minutes and listened, straining my ears with the effort. I could hear the sound of my own heart throbbing as I held my breath.

Once, I thought I heard something walking, crunching twigs and earth way down below me, but my poor over-wrought brain could be playing tricks on me now.

I thought I could hear the footsteps below me as I walked, but then they seemed to stop only a fraction of a second after I halted. Was I only imagining this? The only other sound was the river roaring way off in the distance, like a continuously sighing breeze. No birds tweeting, no insects buzzing, like the silence of the day after the Apocalypse.

"I didn't really hear that howling sound, did I? Was it some sort of weird atmospheric effect warping the sound of the train whistle? No way...it was way too close. What the hell was it?" my thoughts were running rampant. "Why in the hell was a full grown sow bear running panicked towards a human?"

I alternated between trying to explain it to myself rationally, and wild imaginings of ancient beasts from some old medieval painting. I was getting myself more and more wound up, and I started making mistakes, tripping on the rocks in the trail.

I finally had to force myself to relax a little and just walk, as I was wearing myself out with the effort of trying to hear the sounds in the distance, and walk noiselessly at the same time.

I was still nearly three good miles from the first clearing I had picked out on the map, and the sun was now sinking towards the western horizon at what seemed like an alarming rate. The trees had long, dark shadows now, and the only consolation was that the air was a little cooler than it had been. I knew that this coolness would soon turn to real cold, and I would need to be camped by then.

I had no idea what I was going to do once I was there. I would have to set up my little tent and unroll my sleeping bag inside of it. I would have to get warm clothes on and build a fire, or at least get my little gas stove going for hot tea (as I mentioned, open fires were banned in the Wilderness).

All of this was normal operating procedure for a normal day, but it seemed far off and fantastical to me now.

But what was I going to do if that thing—whatever it was—followed me? What could it be, anyway? Would it try to hurt me? What about the bear? Like I said, all I had to defend myself was the can of bear spray—a sort of mace in a large spray bottle that could shoot a full thirty feet away, but it only contained a few shots at that rate. I would be totally defenseless after that, and maybe then with an angry giant on my hands. My only other defense was the few M80s I still had left, and they weren't much to try to defend one's self with—just big firecrackers in essence.

Even though I was in a hurry, I decided it might be a good idea to have the bear spray handy, so I stopped once again to dig it out of my pack, tying one of the water bottles I held in my hand to the rope that held the others so I could hang onto the spray instead of the water.

I also checked the bone again, all the while realizing how obsessed I was becoming with it.

I finally tied that damned clanking pan down tight so I wouldn't have to listen to it any more. My backpack was even heavier now, with the water bottle tied to it—but at least I could hear a little better with the clanking pan now silenced.

I kept on walking as fast as I could up the rocky trail, now with the bear spray in one hand. I started to trip over roots and bumps on the trail again, as it had begun to grow even darker in the shadows of the big pines, and I could no longer see where I was stepping.

Plus, I was already feeling really tired again. Carrying this weight was getting old, especially up these steep switchbacks, and especially in a semi-panic, with the adrenaline now wearing off and leaving me totally exhausted, in spite of the long nap I had had earlier.

FIVE: A RESTLESS NIGHT

I finally came over a small rise and found a nice little spot in a small clearing under a ring of tall Ponderosas. This place would do, and I considered it a godsend, especially under the circumstances. There was even a nice flat boulder—handy to have for a table of sorts—sitting next to a good, level tent site. It wasn't much, but it would have to do.

I kicked the pinecones and small branches off of the flat, grassy spot, and I untied my tent from the rear of the backpack. I pulled it out of its stuff sack and unrolled it, proceeding to hammer in the little aluminum stakes and setting up the fiberglass poles, pulling the nylon of the tent snug.

In a few minutes I had a shelter, such as it was—but it didn't really look like it was much of a safe haven. I unpacked my bag and my sleeping pad and laid them out inside the tent. I could now bed down for the night, and with very little time to spare, as the sun had already sunk beneath the western horizon.

It would be dark, completely dark, in about forty minutes. The trees that made up the western horizon were black branching zigzags, poking up into the edge of the azure blue sky, which was already getting dark in the east. The brighter stars and planets started to shine here and there, twinkling dimly.

It started to get chilly almost immediately, so I decided it would be best to build a fire—a big fire, even though open fires were banned up here. I started gathering flat rocks for a fire ring, along with some firewood.

I was amazed at how edgy and nervous I was. I jumped at every shadow, and I wished I could just relax.

I was still shaken by the eerie howl and the strange encounter with the bear. That was nearly two hours ago now—I couldn't believe that much time had passed, as it seemed like it had been only ten minutes. Funny how time seems to compress when you are under stress—maybe it has something to do with our inner clocks speeding up relative to outside time.

I thought it would be best to have a fire to scare anything undesirable away, although I had my doubts that this would be enough. I started to grab fallen branches from the forest floor surrounding me, supplementing them with dead branches that hung from the big trees all around me. Each time I broke one off, the loud cracking sound would echo down the mountainside, and I listened carefully for any further noises.

I was now in a definite hurry to get a fire going, as it was getting darker and colder by the minute. I kept freaking myself out, thinking I was seeing things out of the corner of my eye; but when I turned to look, there was nothing except maybe a tree branch swaying in the chilly breeze.

Once I had collected a good pile of dry wood, I started a fire. Its warm glow made me feel immediately better, even though the shadows from its light increased amongst the nearby tall pines. The firelight would also temporarily blind me, so I tried not to stare at it too much, in spite of the comforting effect it gave me. I preferred to be able to see as best I could into the gathering darkness.

This little fire I now had represented an ancient source of human security to me, and although it was somewhat tenuous—needing near-constant attention and feeding to keep it going—it still seemed to stave off the darkness. I had decided to conserve my resources instead of burning all of the wood at once, so I'd built a small fire instead of a big one.

I wondered at how our ancestors were able to live like this, outdoors all of the time. There was never any respite from the brutality and hunger of the Earth before we developed our meager 'civilized' methods of staving its dire necessities off.

No wonder most of the ancients died young—I read somewhere that the average lifespan was about thirty-five years for prehistoric people, based on such things as growth of teeth and bones. Back then, if you were as old as forty, you were definitely an elder of the tribe. There were just too many hazards, and their style of living was just too harsh for them to live very long.

After finally getting more settled in and relaxing a little, I dug the bone out of the big backpack, unwrapping it and looking at it closely. It was definitely a big vertebra, and the processes, or 'wings' were extremely long and delicate. I was surprised they hadn't been broken yet, and I made a mental note to pack it more carefully so that that wouldn't happen.

I wondered again if the thing that had howled down below was following me because of the bone.

Had I disturbed a gravesite? Was the thing trying to get back its relative? What was it, anyway? Nothing I could think of would have made that long, drawn-out wailing howl like that. Unless, maybe...no, it couldn't be.

Bigfoot? No, they didn't exist, right? The thought made me instantly nervous again, and I anxiously looked around myself at the darkness of the woods, searching for eyes shining in the firelight.

I slapped suddenly at an insect biting at my arm, itching and annoying me.

In spite of the cool temperature, mosquitoes had been biting me since I had stopped, so I took out my mosquito repellent and slathered it all over me. "That should keep the little bastards at bay," I thought. A few welts had already appeared on my forearms, and I made a mental note to myself to try not to scratch at them, although they were already itching. I hated the poison of the repellent, but I hated the itchiness even worse.

I got out my little stove and lit it up, intending to heat up some noodles for dinner. I used the stove even though I had a fire going, because it is easier to keep my little pan balanced on it, and the pan doesn't get as sooty that way. The little gas stove had a happy little jet roar to it that made me feel even less anxious. Funny how little things like that can sometimes mean so much, especially when we are in a tense situation.

After eating some food, I felt even better, although my trepidation had not yet completely abated. I stayed up and tended the fire, until I was just too exhausted to continue. Besides, I was running out of fuel, and I wanted to save some for later, should I need it. I let the fire gradually burn out. Embers now glowed red and white amongst the ashes, like a tiny city there, twinkling in the stony fire ring.

I finally crawled wearily into my tent, thinking, "To hell with it. If something is going to get me, let it. I can't stay up any longer—I'm too exhausted."

Later, I kept on waking up, imagining I had heard something outside walking around my tent. I would listen intently, and then finally doze off again, having heard nothing. Whatever had awakened me was now still as death. I had the bone wrapped in the t-shirt by my head, and I checked it, feeling for the hard lump in the shirt. It was still there, as it should have been.

I guess I must have been expecting something terrible to happen. I had to crawl out of my little cocoon a couple of times to pee, and I hated the thought of it, but made myself go—I really had no choice. I shone my flashlight around, feeling very vulnerable.

Above, the stars were shining brilliantly, and the Milky Way hung densely overhead—an amazing view that never disappoints me, regardless of how many times I see it. Camping really does have its perks.

I finally calmed down and got into a deep, dreamless sleep about two or three o'clock in the morning. Even those anxious from battle have to rest sometime.

SIX: THE CREATURE REVEALED

Early the next morning I got up, as I had been laying there for quite a while—needing to go to the bathroom again, but not wanting to get up out of the warm sleeping bag. I exhaled sharply, and I could see my breath—it was that cold. I felt for the bone again, and it was still laying there, a cold lump wrapped in the t-shirt. I forced myself to get up and unzip the flap of the tent, stepping outside.

It was now approaching dawn, with a dark blue light glowing above the peaks to the east, brightening towards the horizon. I decided that I should force myself to get on up the trail, since I was so far behind schedule now. The happenings of yesterday already seemed far away and surreal, like a weird dream.

I turned on my flashlight, and I was relieved to see that everything was as I had left it last night—my backpack still swung from the rope where I had hoisted it into a tree, above the reach of the bear. The only accessible bear food was myself, and I had slept with another M80 handy next to my pillow, along with the bear spray—just in case.

I was amazed to see the fire still smoldering a little, with a long blue-white trail of smoke rising up into the air. I got out the gas stove and prepared some instant coffee—an exquisite delicacy way out here, so far away from civilization. I was warming up now, and I didn't feel too bad, in spite of yesterday's bizarreness and the subsequent sleep deprivation.

After eating some cereal mixed with powdered milk and sugar, I lowered the pack and re-packed all of my gear, putting the bone deep inside my extra clothing, where it wouldn't accidentally get broken.

I did an idiot check—where one looks all around just before walking away to make sure one isn't forgetting something—and finally continued plodding on up the dewy trail. It wasn't long before my lower pant legs were wet from where they brushed up against the wet grasses drooping over the edges of the trail.

I should have stopped and put on my gaiters—zippered waterproof nylon leggings that keep the lower pant legs from getting wet—but I decided to just keep going. I had taken too long to get here as it was.

The first thing I noticed was that the songbirds were back now—a wood thrush had awakened me long before the sun was up, a pine warbler soon joined in, and now a robin sang its early morning trill as I walked away from my impromptu camp. It seemed as all was once more well with the world, and yesterday's weirdness was all behind me.

The blue light of dawn was now crossing the entire heavens, and the stars were fading out one by one, as the sun extinguished them with its light. It was an exquisite brisk morning, the start of what looked to be a beautiful day.

Not a cloud could be seen, but the steep walls of the mountains and canyons hid part of the sky. It was much closer from one tall jagged horizon to the other tall jagged horizon, as opposed to horizons that were far away from each other and flatter—like out on the prairie, for example. A storm could be lurking just a few miles over, and I wouldn't be able to see it until it was nearly overhead. Bad weather is notorious for sneaking up on you in the mountains.

I was soon out of the trees, looking up at the peaks for the first time, the view unblocked now by the dense stands of trees and underbrush I had been walking for miles to get through. The sun finally broke over the edge of the eastern horizon and I could feel its sudden radiating warmth. Soon I had to shed the fleece jacket I had been wearing.

I had a surge of excitement as I realized the enormity of what I was about to do—climb some of the most inaccessible and amazing peaks in the United States. Spires of beautiful gray and brown granite rose up to the sky all around me, splattered with green patches of verdant tundra. Snowfields still clung tenuously to the shadows, where the daytime sun couldn't get to them to melt them away.

For those who have never felt the rush of mountain climbing—even non-technical mountain climbing—I must say that you are missing out on one of the most incredible experiences a human being can ever have. Sir Edmund Hillary once said we must climb the mountain because it is there, and I think a more succinct way of putting it has never been uttered.

After a couple of hours, I decided I must stop for a while and just enjoy the landscape. I no longer felt the anxiety of yesterday, and I felt like it was finally time to take it easy. I feel very driven in most of my active life, but I insist that I stop and smell the roses once in awhile.

This place reminded me of photos I had seen of the High Sierras in California. I have always wanted to follow in John Muir's footsteps, and I made a mental note to myself to be sure and go there someday—something I have yet to do.

I took off my backpack once more, and I pulled out my daypack and my little film camera. I immediately started taking pictures. I was suddenly inspired, and I took about thirty-six pictures (a full roll—this was before digital cameras) as I wandered around the meadow I was in, entranced with the beauty of the place. When you've slogged your way through the shadows, you may suddenly find yourself looking up at the sunlit sky. For a few minutes, I forgot about the bone in my backpack, and I think I was a little better off for it.

There was now a small herd of twelve Rocky Mountain goats scattered on the pass up to Chicago Basin, which was still above me. They acted like they were tame, and they started ambling down towards me. I was elated, and I waited patiently as they came close enough to get plenty of decent shots of them.

I made a mental note to be careful not to use up all of my film—I had only six rolls with me, and three of those were still in my big pack below. I had just burned through two rolls already.

One of the big rams got a little skittish as I got a little bit too close for comfort. He reared back like he was going to butt me just as I took a picture. I immediately stepped back a few feet, and he relaxed a little.

But I managed to get a fabulous shot of him with his front legs reared up in the air, as if defying gravity, with the gorgeous sunlit peaks behind him. I had the photo enlarged and framed when I got back home, and it now adorns the wall above my desk at home—definitely one of my favorite memories.

I soon got burned out on my short-felt elation. After putting away the little camera, I slammed some water and decided to shoulder the backpack once again. I should get on up into Chicago Basin, still a couple of miles further on—up a rocky pass, where I would make my base camp up above tree line at about 12,500 feet above sea level.

I would be totally exposed up there if the weather should get nasty, but I didn't care. This was part of why I came up here—to challenge myself and break out of my comfort zone.

I was feeling much better about life than I was yesterday, and I had forgotten the strange things that had happened, like they had been part of an old sepia-toned photo in a museum parlor in some Colorado mountain ghost town. It all really seemed like just a strange dream at this point.

I was now in fine form all of a sudden, my lungs were clear and deep, and the clear mountain breeze that now burst down from the peaks up above gave me a sense of new adventure as I breathed it happily in. I was feeling acclimated, finally.

I was now at the head of the valley, looking up at the steep trail that leads up to Twin Lakes, two high-mountain tarns nestled in uppermost Chicago Basin, at the foot of the three Fourteeners, Mt. Eolus, Windom Peak, and Sunlight Peak. The wind suddenly gusted coldly from the rocky tundra up the narrow little trail, as if in acknowledgement of my high-altitude musings.

The wind made me a little anxious, and I suddenly decided instead to set up camp here—at the base of the pass—where there were still some big trees for shelter and security. Up above, at Twin Lakes, it looked like there was only bare rock, at least according to the map, and I didn't want to be too exposed, even though I had been in situations like that before. If there were a big lightning storm, I might regret it. Some clouds abruptly passed across the sun, chilling the air and underscoring my trepidation.

I set up my camp, pitching the little tent snugly under one of the tall Ponderosas, and I got out the folding lean-to chair I had bought in Boulder just last week to test it for comfort. I was sick and tired of not having something to lean back against when I went camping. I found it amazingly comfortable, in spite of it not having a proper seat.

Anyway, I had set up my camp and got into my lunch bag, eating some potted tuna fish salad and crackers, along with some raisins and some dried bananas, when I looked up at the patchy snow-covered expanse of the bowl of Twin Lakes Basin above me. The sky had grown grayer now, and clouds were scudding at the tops of the peaks above me.

As I looked, I noticed a dark spot there in the face of the upper cirque, an odd-looking black speck there in the patchy snowfields that often remained all summer, never melting off at this altitude because they were in shadow most of the time. The peaks beyond were amazing—giant quartzite spires, pointing straight up into the sky above the bowl. I was going to go up there tomorrow, if all went well.

I got my 30X monocular out of my pack, and looked at the strange blotch up on the slope. I could now see that it was a big shelter cave, formed by the abutting of three big slabs of broken down stone, making an entrance in a triangular shape in the middle of the enormous snow-covered talus slope. I couldn't see very far into it, as the angle of the lighting was not quite right. But it looked like it might be a sizeable shelter. "Could be a life-saver in bad weather," I made a mental note to myself.

As if on cue, the wind suddenly blasted down the shoulder of Mt. Eolus to my immediate west, hitting me with a sudden chill, and causing the tent flaps to slap noisily around. I finished the tuna fish, then went around and made sure once again that the stakes and ropes were adequately secured. I tapped a couple of them into the ground, as they had already worked their way loose in the wind. The ground here was rocky and it was hard to get a good purchase in with the little triangular aluminum stakes. I stacked rocks on them to help secure them better.

I shivered, thinking this must be the beginning of the storm the television news had forecast for this area. It had looked like maybe a few days of rain, but beyond that who knows? The weather forecasts were only about five days accurate, if that. I hoped it wouldn't get too crappy, and I was even more relieved that I had stopped hiking before completely leaving the tree line for the barren rock above me.

I turned to get into my backpack for a sweater I carry, when a definite flash of light caught my eye, off to my far right in a group of trees down slope from me. Something had moved in the shadows down there, something that was whiter than the darkness surrounding it.

It must have been fairly large for me to see it from this distance, as I was about two hundred yards up the hill. It was down in a copse of about twenty or thirty small pine trees that was a little set apart from the main body of the dark forest further behind it, down the hill.

I squinted, holding my breath to still myself better. Nothing moved, and I wore out my eyes with squinting. My heart rate increased. I immediately remembered the bone again, and I had to stop myself from checking on it—it was where I had left it, I was certain.

I breathed out, and reached down, grabbing my monocular again. I peered through it, holding my breath again. There! Something had moved back to the right in the shadows, a vague brightness that was quickly lost in the shade. It was as if it had seen me look away, using my momentary lapse of attention as a point of quick escape.

It disappeared swiftly into the bigger, darker forest behind—a definite white streak amidst the dark shadows that the trees cast in the early afternoon sun. I wondered if it had been a skunk, but the angles seemed all wrong, as if it had been floating weirdly above the ground. Besides, I was too far away for a skunk to have grabbed my attention—unless it was one really big skunk.

The hackles were up on my neck suddenly, and I suddenly remembered the eerie howl and the frightened bear, all of which had propelled me hastily up the trail yesterday. I was instantly aware of my total aloneness, and I felt suddenly isolated, exposed, and vulnerable.

I checked for the bear spray in my pack, and I got another M80 ready in my shirt pocket. I was fidgeting a little now, and I felt nervous. My intuition was suddenly keyed up, and I instinctively knew to be cautious.

I rarely feel this way, but when I do, I pay attention, because any time I have ever ignored it, something bad usually happens.

I now shivered even more, and I finally pulled out the sweater and put it on. My sweat had turned cold, and I was keenly aware of the need for warmth. The temperature was considerably colder now than it had been since early this morning, and I felt a foreboding like something bad was going to happen. The sky was getting cloudier and darker now, and the wind was stronger and colder.

I checked the bone again, nestled down in the extra change of clothing I had brought. It was still there, safe. I shivered a little in spite of the sweater, and I knew I needed to get warm before I lost any more of my body heat. I decided I'd better have some hot tea, then get everything ready in case it really did start to storm.

The trees were sighing and beginning to bend with the wind a little, and I figured that if this turned out to be a big storm, it would probably be preceded by big downdrafts of strong winds—so I had better batten everything down. I dragged my big pack into the tent, its weight a surety against the tent blowing away. "It would take a hurricane to blow that hulk away," I thought.

I tied my tent more securely to the big tree it was under, hoping there wouldn't be any lightning strikes here, where everything I owned could become incinerated. I guess you have to take risks to get anywhere in this world, and there really isn't any definite security—only mitigated probabilities.

Anyway, I got out the rest of my cold weather clothes, pulling on a wool cap and shoving my parka and long johns into the tent for convenience, where I had earlier laid out my bag and pad. At least I could climb inside, get warm, and ride out the storm if I had to. I had rain gear, too, and I pulled it out, putting on the jacket and stuffing the pants where I could easily reach them in the top of my daypack.

The sinking feeling I had in my gut returned now, as the few trees around me roared in another blast of cold wind coming from the west, dropping needles and pine cones from the lower branches, landing on my tent and sliding down to the ground.

The nylon flapped madly in the gusting wind, and sand and dirt stung my face. It started to rain a little, and I leaned over and looked at my watch. It was only two o'clock, and the prospect of spending the entire afternoon hunkered down in my tent was a bit depressing. It was still at least six hours until sundown, and that was too much time to spend staring at the inside of the blue and yellow walls of my tent, with nothing to do to pass the time.

I decided I was going to try to do some looking around in spite of the wind, at least in the surrounding area. I didn't want to stray too far from my tent, though. I got up and grabbed a water jug, along with my camera, which I put in my rain jacket pocket where it would be handy.

The wind blew another rainy blast, and I wondered if I were crazy to even think about leaving my little shelter. I changed my mind and got the rain pants out, putting them on. I put on my daypack—with water, first aid, emergency food, and survival gear in it—and I walked out of the little campsite, going up the trail a ways, trying to get a little above the trees for a better view out.

I stopped again, turning around. The bone was still in the big backpack, and I was compelled to dig it out and take it with me, in case someone (or something) came along and stole it. If I had it on me at all times, this couldn't happen, I reasoned. I walked back down to my camp, and I got it out of the big pack in the tent. I shoved it gently down into the daypack, under my survival pack on the bottom.

It was raining continuously now as I walked back up the trail, but at least the wind had died down a bit. The light rain spattered noisily on my rain parka, but it wasn't enough to get me very wet. I would stay pretty dry, anyway, with all of my rain gear on. My boots were waterproof also, so I wasn't too worried about the rain.

I crossed under a talus slope to the west of the trail, where broken down plates of rock had collected from the enormous eroding steep slopes above. I then went off trail, up the rocky tundra slope to the east, to get a better vantage point of the valley far below me.

There was a little crag that stood out from the rest of the slope, less than a half-mile upslope from me. I knew I could get a better view from up there, so I clambered clumsily up the rough slope, slipping and tripping occasionally on the tumbled down scree.

The loose rocks made it hard going, and I was glad I had on heavy-duty hiking boots, as the stones would have injured my toes, falling on them. It was 'one step forward, two steps back' for a while.

After about twenty minutes of this, I finally arrived at the "little" crag—it turned out to be about forty feet tall—and I climbed around the side of it to get up on top.

I could now see Needle Creek below me—a tiny white ribbon of water dashing here and there on the exposed rocks, shining and contrasting with the overcast, darker landscape—before disappearing into the chasm below in the deeper, shadowy forest.

The wind gusted at me again, blowing cold raindrops at me and making me almost lose my balance as I stood on the edge of the crag. I decided I had better sit down for a bit.

I looked back down at the valley below me and was astonished to see what looked like a person coming up the watercourse of Needle Creek—the steepest part of the valley, and therefore the hardest to climb up. "Why doesn't he just use the trail?" I thought to myself.

Then I realized that what I was seeing couldn't possible be a man, as it looked way too big, coming rapidly up the creek bottom. I felt the goose bumps rise on my arms as I watched. The hackles were suddenly up in full force on my neck again.

Whatever it was, it was very agile, especially for something that big. It leapt from rock to rock and from stream bank to stream bank, without pausing, like it had been practicing the route and had it all memorized.

It was now only about five hundred vertical feet below me, and I could see it clearly for the first time as it stepped into a clearing amidst some tall brush.

It was standing on a portion of the trail, next to one of the tall willows in a narrower part of the valley, one I remembered walking past earlier. I remember the willows being about ten feet tall—I had considered camping there, and I was watching for a good place to hang my food cache out of the reach of bears, so I had taken notice of them. But willows are way too springy to hold much weight, so I had ignored them after noting how tall they were, especially at this high altitude—about 11,000 feet above sea level—where plants tend instead to be dwarfed.

Now I couldn't believe my eyes. The person—or whatever it was—looked almost as tall as the willows were, at least from up here. I quickly pulled out my little monocular again, wondering if I had really seen it correctly, thinking maybe that I had mistaken how big it was.

The monocular was now fogged with humidity, so I dried it quickly on my shirttail, aggravated at the delay.

But I was immediately astonished to see that it was very much like a really big man. It loped along like a big man, and it stood upright like a big man—except it was totally unlike any man—big or otherwise—that I've ever seen.

Like I said, it walked upright like a man, but the arms were a lot longer, actually hanging down a little past the level of its knees. It was dark black, covered with bushy dark hair, and it looked like a lanky gorilla, with big flared nostrils and a sharp ridge of thicker hair running down the length of the top of its head—no doubt where strong jaw muscles attached to the ridge of the skull.

It walked easily along, and it leaped casually what must have been ten feet across the stream bed in one place, as it came striding rapidly up the valley.

Its long black hair was hanging down from all along its body, and I guessed the hair was probably about a foot long along the sides and the arms where the back lighting showed it in fine detail. It was stringy and really thick.

The thing had been looking up toward my camp—down below me—but then it suddenly looked straight up the slope at me, like it had sensed me looking at it, abruptly surprised to see me up here instead of at the little camp-site, where it had been intently staring a moment before. I distinctly saw the change in the angle of its eyes—that's how close the image appeared in the monocular.

Its deep dark glistening eyes looked straight through me, as if melting the little glass monocular I was holding, probing deep into my soul. I was startled, and I looked away for a second, past the little scope—shocked at what I had been looking at. The hair stood up on my neck, and my entire skin tingled with trepidation. Goose bumps instantly stood up on my arms.

By the time I had the monocular back to my eye, the beast had already turned around, as if in an abrupt panic, and it strode evenly but quickly down the rocky slope, looking occasionally over its shoulder back up at me, un-til it entered a stand of big trees just a couple of hundred yards below my campsite, but across the stream from where I was now. It had only taken half a minute to cross three hundred yards of uneven, rocky terrain. Then it was gone again, into the deep shadows.

When the creature had turned around to leave, I spotted what I had seen only vaguely a couple of times before—I just hadn't known what it was that I was looking at then: a big silver-white stripe that adorned the back of its black head, from the crest all the way midway down its back, shining in the overcast daylight, like a white mane.

This is what I had thought had been a skunk earlier. The silver stripe was clearly visible, even in the shadows of the big trees, until the thing disappeared into the deeper shadows, and for some reason it reminded me of the Cheshire Cat's lingering smile in Alice in Wonderland—but the smile now seemed somehow rotten and malignant, and the thought made me feel suddenly ill.

I think my poor brain was just trying to latch onto anything that might be of comfort, and I even grinned sickly to myself at the image, in spite of the shock that was now upwelling inexorably into my awareness.

Now I blanched, the blood racing out of my head and leaving me feeling very light-headed and dizzy. I was glad I was sitting down—falling up here could easily become a catastrophe, with nobody here to help me if I became injured.

I suddenly became keenly aware of how fleeting life is, and I leaned over a little backwards on the palms of my hands, with my arms now stretched out behind me. I looked up at the gray, overcast sky, and the cold rain fell into my eyes.

I realized that I was trapped up here in the wilderness with the biggest wild animal I had ever seen, and the first one I had ever seen that could stand on two legs and walk like a huge giant of a man. My heart was now pounding in my chest, and I was breathing in shallow gasps of air.

I was acutely terrified, and I didn't know what to do. It had obviously seen me, then startled away swiftly, as if I had surprised it in the course of a crime. But then again, I had probably inadvertently scared it with the M80 I threw at the bear yesterday, and maybe it thought I had a gun up here with me. I could potentially shoot it from way up here if I did, couldn't I? Did it know all of this? Was this an intelligent creature?

Obviously, it was, and this thought terrified me even more.

Had this thing been trying to sneak up on me, whatever it was? I had read some fanciful Bigfoot stories when I was younger, but I had dismissed them as just that, fanciful fiction. Now I was quick in realizing what it was that I had seen—this was definitely not a bear, nor a man, nor was it like anything I have ever seen. I'd only heard of this, and only seen it in a couple of cheesy old Bigfoot movies and television shows. I'd assumed the whole thing was just a hoax—until now.

This was a Bigfoot and I had seen it in vivid detail, every wrinkle of its face, every matted tress of its long hair. I had even noticed the steam coming from its nostrils, condensing in the humid, chilly mountain air.

I was now forever shocked by the sudden upset of my once placid world. I was no longer under any pretense of security, and my mountain refuge had become the haven of devils. I had no protection whatsoever from such a beast, especially if it wanted to do me harm—there would be no contest, and I would lose.

Whatever that thing was, it seemed to have been heading for my camp down below, where my big backpack was—and that is where I had earlier stashed the bone.

The bone! I had somehow known I had to carry the bone up here with me! Of course, it was after the bone! Why else would it be trying to creep up on me like that? It wanted the bone back!

The realization of what this might mean stunned me. I had accidentally picked up a Bigfoot vertebra! I now had scientific proof that Bigfoot existed! And I knew exactly where the creature's 'grave' was—I had carefully marked it on the topo map, in case it might turn out to be an important find, and I would have to come back to it again later.

I compulsively reached down into my daypack, feeling for the bone in its wrapping. Still there, a cold hardness wrapped in the clothing.

The awareness of my discovery swiftly dawned on me as I blinked the rain from my eyes, wondering if I had been dreaming somehow. It was like I had been suddenly transported into an alien realm, beyond the grasp of my feeble imagination.

I reeled as I scanned the horizon around and above me. I looked intently for a few minutes up in the shadows of the gray cliffs around the head of the cirques above me, straining my vision to detect any movements up there.

What if there were more of them? Had I violated their sacred ground by stealing the bone?

My life had been instantly and forever altered by the last few moments, and I had seen something that just a few seconds ago I would have argued didn't even exist. I was in a state of profound shock, and I reeled at the enormity of it. I was at a total loss what to do.

But I was in no position to be leisurely or complacent, because the wind now whipped furiously down the mountainside, sandblasting my face again with little grains. The rain now began to come down in painful, pelting big drops. I zipped up my raincoat and pulled the hood tighter around my face.

I have never felt so exposed and vulnerable in my life, except once, as a ten-year-old child, when my father had left me alone in the woods to go get a deer he had bagged. He had said he would be right back, but it seemed like an eternity, and I had felt momentarily abandoned to the wilds, like Oedipus as a baby, abandoned on the rocks for the wolves to eat.

I know now that I had been forever scarred by this incident, and it didn't come to me until later that there was a lot more to what had happened than just the few details I had remembered before.

As I brought this memory to mind, I got a strange angst in my soul, and I suddenly felt that I would be dying soon, very soon. The existential pain of life, along with my exhaustion, suddenly hit me. Tears welled up in my eyes, and I started sobbing uncontrollably. I shuddered and rocked back and forth with the emotional pain for a few minutes, but then I finally bucked up and got my breath.

This was really freaking me out, and I had to pull myself together. This was no place to turn into a basket case.

I now realized that I had a heavy psychological burden I must rid myself of, and for the first time it finally occurred to me now what the nature of that burden might be: I had already seen a Bigfoot so many years ago.

I had seen one when I was just ten, and my dad had abandoned me, leaving me alone and exposed to it. I had always thought that he had left me in my hour of need, and the thought made me tear up and sob again for a few seconds. But now I remember exactly what happened so many years ago, and I now realized that he wasn't to blame.

But now, the wind was whipping furiously around me, and I must get back to my camp, even if that thing was still down there, waiting for me. My only option for staying warm was down there, along with the rest of my food and water. I had no choice but to return the way I had come, or freeze to death up here.

Once more, my face was stung by flying sand and dirt, literally sandblasted by the wind. I had to quickly grab my daypack before it toppled off the edge of the crag I had been sitting on, knocked over suddenly by the ferocity of the wind.

Then sleet came abruptly in hard, biting, freezing needles, and the wind gusted nearly horizontally at my face. I realized that the only shelter I had up here in this foreboding place was now nearly a mile below me. I had to get back to my tent, in spite of what I'd seen down there. There,

I had supplies and a stove to get myself warm. I started to shiver violently, and I had to force myself to stand up and shoulder the daypack, before it was too late.

I would just get wetter and freeze to death if I stayed here very much longer. I was already shivering, but I wondered if some of that was from fear. The sun was now ebbing surely towards the west, and the gray of the clouds near the eastern horizon became a deeper gray, tending towards the color of night. I couldn't sit here for much longer.

I steeled myself to do what I had to do, and I forced myself to drink some more water—it's easier to get dehydrated when the weather is cold, because you aren't as aware of your lack of water as you are when it is hot outside. I made sure I was no longer dizzy, breathing in deeply, deliberately, and slowly. I prepared to leave my perch on the crag.

I started walking carefully back down to the trail. The loose rocks I had crossed earlier had the added hazard of being wet now, so I deliberately took my time, even though the storm was now roaring all around me, with stinging volleys of sand and sleet hitting me in the face from time to time.

I was in the main downdraft of what must be a pretty good storm rolling in from the west. The treetops down below were whipping around now, and I could hear their sighing in the wind. I hoped fervently that my tent was still firmly anchored.

Suddenly, I felt a surge of energy. I guess the adrenaline kicked in, because I only vaguely remember the crazy, freezing, windy walk back down—I only know that it seemed to take no time at all, and I was suddenly back at my camp.

The adrenaline from the emotional trauma had sustained me, and I was operating now on autopilot. I vaguely remember being extremely careful with each and every step, all the while nearly running down the mountain at full speed. You'd be amazed what you can do under heavy stress.

Fortunately, my tent was still secure, and nothing had blown away. The weight of my big backpack had kept the tent firmly on the ground.

As I stood there, panting with exertion, I pondered getting all of my gear together and just high-tailing it out of there, but it was now late afternoon, and it was raining and sleeting hard—plus, it was getting really cold.

There was no way I could make it the six miles back down to the river before sundown, and slogging out in a rainstorm in the dark would not only be a drag—it would be dangerous, even with a flashlight. It would be too easy to lose the trail and get lost, or slip and twist an ankle, or something even worse.

Besides all of this, the train didn't run this time of day, and I would have to camp out down below anyway, until it arrived at about eleven o'clock the next morning. I had at least eighteen hours before I could get safely on the train, so I decided instead to just wait it out up here, in spite of my trauma and trepidation.

It seemed to be the only sane option I had left—although I now felt as if all sanity had abandoned me. Running never seemed like the right thing to do, especially up here where the least little misstep could lead to injury and disaster—with all probability of it ending in death.

At least this way, I stood a chance, however terrifying. Maybe the thing would leave me alone somehow. I wondered weirdly if I had picked up the vertebra of one of its relatives, and how would I feel if it had been a relative of mine?

It had now grown really cold, and I could see my breath. I nervously glanced down the valley towards the stand of trees the creature had disappeared into. I decided that I would again light a small fire if I only could, in spite of the wilderness restrictions. I had to get warm, and I had to have some sort of defense against the thing, even if it was only a psychological one. A fire might just scare it away, if I was lucky. I nervously fingered the M80 in my shirt pocket, making sure it was still there.

I gathered some dry firewood from underneath the big trees nearby, cautiously looking over my shoulder every few seconds. I kept the daypack on while I worked, knowing the bone was still in there, not wanting to be apart from it.

I now fully expected something terrible to happen to me, and I imagined the newspaper headline: 'Man Vanishes Without a Trace in Wilderness'—I would become just another statistic. I again gathered some flat rocks to use for a fire ring, arranging them in a crude circle.

The little fire I finally got going in spite of everything being wet seemed like nothing that would scare off the likes of the big creature, but it did cheer me up a little nonetheless. I had to be careful, though, because it was under the big lower limb of one of the Ponderosas, out of the intermittent sleet and rain, but where it could possibly kindle the tree if I weren't watchful.

After a while, the cold sleet turned into a light snow for a while, and I knew I was in for a long cold night. But at least the wind had died down a little. I built up the little fire as best I could under the dripping branch of the tree, being extremely careful not to start the tree on fire. I would have to carefully feed the little fire almost continuously with the damp wood to keep it going, and I knew it would quickly die out as soon as I went to bed.

I also got my little stove purring and after a few minutes drank some hot tea, which warmed me considerably, making me feel a little better. It was only five o'clock by my watch, and I knew it would be a long, cold time until sunrise—thirteen hours or so. Even though it was still daylight out, it felt dark and gloomy in the sleet and snow.

The clouds along the western horizon now became a bright gray, and I knew the sun was still shining up above them—a small consolation. I was still all keyed up, and I peered through the sleety drizzle in all directions, intently watching for movement. I jumped at every little sound, like a couple of times when the fire popped especially loudly.

Sunset was still a few hours away. I gathered a bunch more firewood, which was easy to find since nobody had been using it up here, with the rules and all: no open fires, period. I think it was a hundred-dollar fine back then if you got caught. I didn't care, and I surmised that any judge would concur with my actions, given the circumstances. The entire time I looked nervously around, expecting imminent doom.

I ate a meal of ramen noodles and a hard roll with some tuna, drinking it all down with hot Jello (my favorite camp drink). I decided the best thing to do was to just try to stay calm, as if nothing had happened.

After several hours of just sitting there, trying to stay warm and feeding the fire, I finally hunkered down into my sleeping bag in the tent, exhausted. Hopefully I was ready enough for a long, cold night.

Even though I was still worried about the bone—it sat wrapped in the t-shirt next to my head again now—I finally dozed off.

SEVEN: THE LONG NIGHT

That night was one of the longest I have ever had to suffer through. Not because of the beast—I didn't hear a peep out of it. I think the weather was too crappy, and it probably had to hide out in its own form of shelter, presumably down there somewhere in the trees. Somewhere far away from me, I hoped.

For my part, I thought more than once that I was going to freeze to death, and I had to get up twice to heat tea and warm myself up. I simply hadn't brought enough warm clothing, and I was on the edge of hypothermia. I had everything on now—my long johns, my sweater, my jeans, my wool cap, my gloves, plus my parka and rain pants. It was still too damn cold. I could see my breath in the air as I exhaled.

All of that clothing made it hard to get comfortable, as it would bunch up when I rolled over, cutting off the circulation in my arms and legs. I had to straighten it to pull it out of my groin and armpits. I finally had to take off the bulky parka once I got a little warmer, as it was only making things worse.

Besides, the wool cap covered up my ears, and I can't sleep very well when I can't hear what is going on around me—especially when I need to listen for Bigfoot.

I woke up many times shivering, finally knowing that I had to somehow get warm—that was the first time I got up and lit the stove. I had let the little fire finally go out, as it was just too difficult to keep it going in the snow. It had smoldered and steamed for a while, with the snow hissing as it hit the hot embers.

Yes, snow. It was snowing big time now. I had to lift the sagging roof of the nylon tent up several times to keep it from pushing down on me from the snow weight. I was getting claustrophobic in addition to everything else.

I was getting really nervous now, but I had all but forgotten the Bigfoot. The weather was the main threat at this point.

I had named the Bigfoot 'Silver' for the big streak of silver hair running down its neck. I guess it takes away some of the mystery of things when we name them, allowing us to categorize them somehow in our minds.

Funny, the name reminded me of the Lone Ranger's horse, and any humor I could think of was very welcome now. "Hi-ho, Silver, awayyyy!!" I chuckled ironically to myself. I only wished it would go away. Maybe it would, of its own accord. One could always hope.

But really, I was way more concerned with keeping from freezing to death than another Bigfoot encounter. I had foolishly allowed myself to get a little wet earlier, after taking off my rain gear. Now I was paying dearly for it, shivering fitfully.

I thought at one point in the middle of the night that I heard some grunts and growls down the valley a ways from me, waking me abruptly. I listened intently, holding my breath.

But I didn't hear it again. Everything had grown serenely quiet in the falling snow, and I could hear tree branches cracking above me from the snow weight. Once in awhile, one would pop loudly below me in the stand of trees where I had last seen the creature.

Again I woke up in terror, listening intently for anything else. Nothing. I finally got back to sleep after about ten or fifteen minutes, too exhausted to care—after checking on the bone, of course. Still there.

Then the cold woke me up again. I didn't get a lot of good sleep that night, needless to say, and I was frustrated and exhausted beyond words.

At one point, when I got up the second time to heat tea, I shone my flashlight upwards into the big Ponderosa I was under, wondering if the branches would break, burying me in snow. But the big tree looked about as safe as it could— at least as far as I could tell under the circumstances. The wind had finally died out entirely, leaving only a deathly silence for the icy snow to fall into. Even so, it was so cold!

After several hours, I finally got dry enough in my bag to actually get warm. My body heat had finally forced the dampness in my clothes out into the atmosphere. I now slept a little better, but now I was having strange dreams.

I dreamed I was back up in the cave—I now realized even in my sleep that this was the shelter cave I had spotted earlier in the day—but something was wrong—very, very wrong.

It was summer, and the now warm breeze blew up from the sighing valley beneath me, carrying on it the acrid smell of something big burning—the forest below. My eyes were watering from the poisonous blue and brown smoke. There was no place to escape the stench, and I gagged on it, coughing and hacking.

But at least now I was finally warm, so very warm. I lay down in the dirt of the cave, as the smoke billowed into the opening. I was ready to sleep now, to forever cast off the anguish of life. I grasped the bone, wrapped tightly in the snowshoe hare's skin.

Now something enormously loud and weirdly alien to me flew up suddenly from the inferno below, and it soared overhead, a big bucket on a cable trailing a stream of water behind and below it.

I was now suddenly standing abruptly outside the door of the cave, looking up into the sky, and it was filled with a brown, sickening, smoky daylight, like what must have been the death pall of Pompei. I clutched the hareskin with the bone in it tightly in my right hand.

The helicopter flew on over the pass between Mt. Eolus and Sunlight Peak, but I didn't know I knew the word 'helicopter'—and 'Eolus' and 'Sunlight' were not the names I used for the two mountains. How I knew this, I couldn't tell. It was as if I inhabited two bodies at once, and the realization of this shocked me suddenly. I was now really awake.

I immediately became acutely claustrophobic, as the snow had settled once more on the tent roof, pressing it down into my face. I pushed it off, and it slid off the nylon with a 'whoosh'. Apparently I hadn't tightened the tent's straps adequately. I now realized that it was getting lighter outside, and I looked at the watch I had stashed above me, in the tent's interior webbing.

I pushed the light button on the watch. It was 5:42 A.M.—still a little early. I really didn't want to leave my now luxuriously warm cocoon. I could see my breath as I exhaled, condensing into ice, and I really didn't want to have to climb out into the frigid air.

But I had to pee, and I just couldn't put it off any longer. I had had too many cups of tea trying to stay warm last night. I obsessively checked on the bone again, as if it could grow legs and walk away from me, or dissipate strangely into the air somehow. It was still there.

I resignedly unzipped my sleeping bag, put on the leather sandals I used for camp shoes over my thick wool socks, and unzipped the little tent, stepping wearily outside.

The ground was now blanketed with about four inches of freshly fallen snow—less than I had imagined—and tree-dropped crystals glinted brilliantly above in the hazy light of the imminent dawn. The western sky was ablaze with the remnants of last night's storm: clouds all pink, blue and yellow, with a fiery red lining the tops of the peaks above me on the western horizon.

What I figured must be Mt. Kennedy—judging from the topo map—was a set of spires of blazing yellow-red light, up on the top of the peaks, where the now clear morning sun must be shining, already beginning to melt the white snow that reflected its brilliant red light—alpenglow—red light that is backscattered and refracted by the atmosphere, reflecting from surfaces on the ground, occurring at sunrise or sunset (contrary to opinion, alpenglow is not actually direct sunlight).

My breath hung in frosty sheets, wafting upward lightly in the slight breeze. My open-toed sandals let my wool socks get a little wet in the melting snow under my toes. I hurried and peed, then immediately got back into the warm sleeping bag in the tent, quickly zipping it up again.

BRRRRR!! I was shivering again now, and I wished I could just go back to sleep for a while. I pulled my wool cap down tighter on my head. My breath hung icily in the air in front of my face, making little clouds that lightly snowed down a bit as they evaporated. I just wanted to sleep some more.

But I lay there for about twenty minutes, and I couldn't doze off due to the cold. I decided that I had better get another hot cup of tea in me, and then some hot instant oatmeal. I was a lot less stressed, now that I knew the sun was rising, and the darkness and cold of last night were hopefully soon to dissipate.

EIGHT: THE EDGE OF THE ABYSS

I soon got the little stove whistling, drinking the hot tea with relief. I now felt much improved, warming up nicely. I made some more hot water and stirred up some instant oatmeal, eating it hungrily.

I put on my boots, got back into my down parka, and walked around the immediate area a bit, to see if I could find any tracks in the snow. Nothing. The snow was pristine. Clumps occasionally slid off of the tree branches down below me, and I could hear them whoosh and thud softly as they hit the ground.

Yesterday's bizarre sighting was like a strange dream now, and I had a newfound energy—in spite of not getting much sleep. I actually wondered for a moment if it had all only been a dream, but I knew deep inside it was real— no denying it. I thought I should probably hightail it out of there, but I really didn't want to leave now—I felt like a new man.

It's odd how the light of day can totally change your perspective, even when times are fretful. Besides, I would have to walk back through the section of forest where— presumably—the beast might lay in wait. That seemed reason enough to stay here.

But I was in the Needles, and I came here to climb, damn it! To hell with it—I would climb, in spite of all that had happened! Besides, the danger up there was probably less than the danger down here. Plus, I had another M80 nestled away in the pocket of my shirt, and the Zippo in my pants pocket, ready for action should anything weird happen.

I wondered if the snow would pose much of a problem, but I knew it would probably melt off soon—after all, it was summer, and it couldn't last for very long. I would only have to wait for the sun to heat up a little.

Even the high peaks would feel the effect of the July sun quickly. Besides, I had crampons and an ice ax—standard gear for protection against sliding should I have to cross any late-season snowfields.

I went around the tent again and tightened all of the stay lines in case the wind should pick up again while I was gone.

I then got my daypack ready—with extra food and my survival kit this time—and I started up the still shadowy, now snowy trail up to Twin Lakes Basin, called Chicago Basin proper on the map.

I took one full water jug and one half-empty one, which I could fill up when I found a good snowmelt stream above. I had iodine to put in it to keep from getting Giardiasis again, although the chances of Giardia up here were slim, as livestock didn't usually go this high. But it was better to be safe than sorry.

The trail was slicker now than it had been yesterday, so it was slow going for a while. My big clunky Vasque mountaineering boots were not necessarily the best rock-gripping shoes, but they were the right choice for the rugged talus and the rivulets of water that now began streaming down the trail—the thick boots were totally waterproof, even if a little bit slippery at times.

It was way too rocky to put on the crampons, as the sharp points would get dull in only a short time. Crampons are mainly for snow and ice—not rocky terrain.

The sun must already be melting things off up above, because as I mentioned the water rivulets were streaming down the trail, eroding it and the massive mountains up above me slowly, grain by grain into Needle Creek below, to be washed eventually into the Animas River, where the train rushes by the rapid water taking its sandy load to the Pacific Ocean—or at least down to Lake Powell, for a geologically short stay.

I went slowly to keep from busting my ephemeral butt on some all-too-permanent rock—definitely not something I wanted to happen. It was only about seven thirty in the morning now, but it already seemed warmer than it had been just an hour ago.

I was now ecstatic to be here, and I sang praises of my good fortune—ironically, I thought, considering the strange occurrences of yesterday. The sun finally burst across the lip of the pass above me, and I could feel its sudden sensate warmth radiating into my jacket and wool hat. I stopped and dug out my sunglasses, a necessity in the high mountains, where the UV rays are much more potent, and where snowfields can give you snow blindness from the reflection on a sunny day.

I was well above the tree line, now, looking back down occasionally to where I had come from—the little patch of trees down there at the head of the valley. I deeply breathed in the thin air, feeling like the torments of the night before had somehow given me new lungs. A little acclimation goes a long ways.

I was now feeling in fine form for some reason—in spite of my sleep deprivation—and I knew I had to take advantage of the feeling while it was still here. The weird happenings of yesterday seemed like eons ago, like some strange archaic story from the myths of the ancients, like Beowulf or the Odyssey.

The moss-covered granite shone wetly through patches of rapidly melting snow in the warm morning sun. Mt. Eolus, at 14,002 feet above sea level, is about 1440 feet higher than the lower Twin Lake, which is itself only a few feet lower than the upper Twin Lake—both Twin Lakes lie in the bottom of a steep bowl, with tundra covered granite ledges going down into the valley, where I now stood.

I needed to watch carefully, or I'd miss the side trail that went up to the lakes. The main trail goes on up to the approach to Windom Peak and Sunlight Peak, the two other Fourteeners to the east of Eolus. The Eolus trail follows a steep creek bed that climbs nearly 1500 feet in less than two miles—hard slogging. There, it tops out at the Twin Lakes bowl, then on up towards the west and the summit above.

It took me about 90 minutes, but I finally topped over the ridge into Twin Lakes Basin, winded and ready for a break. The beautiful lakes both reflected the now azure sky, with only a few little cotton ball cumulus clouds following the trailing edge of last night's big storm.

It was still chilly, especially when the breeze blew up occasionally, so I wore my light rain jacket over my sweater, with my long-john underwear underneath. I was fairly well prepared for the cold, as I also had my fleece jacket tied around the back end of my daypack. Plus, I had my rain gear stowed inside.

The peaks reflected in Twin Lakes looked ethereal—big blocks of smoothly weathered granite and quartzite that shone and glistened in the morning sun, especially where the snowmelt had wetted their solid slopes with runoff streams, like silvery tears. These mirrored the white-hot sun with piercing glares of bright light, sparkling and shimmering on the still waters.

I was glad I had on my sunglasses, keeping me from getting sunburned eyes. The UV rays at this altitude (over two miles above sea level) could easily burn your eyes, as I had once found out from experience—I had climbed for a full sunny summer day without eye protection at altitude on bright snowfields, on Wilson Peak, some 25 miles west of here. My eyes were swollen and in pain for almost a week after that, and I am lucky I didn't do any permanent damage.

I leaped across the little stream at the outflow from the lower Twin Lake. I then climbed up above the east side, up to where the trail to Windom and Sunlight Peak starts. Instead of taking this trail, I climbed across some tundra to where I could see another trail that obviously went up to the upper Twin Lake. I stopped at the upper lake near a big rock that made a small peninsula, jutting into the lake.

I had just started to eat an early lunch (it was 11:00 now) when several Rocky Mountain goats came towards me across the lower slope of Mt. Eolus, to the west. There were eighteen of them—I carefully counted them, and for some reason I still remember the number. I wondered how many of them were the same ones I had seen yesterday, if any.

They watched me from the other side of the little tarn for a while, and then they started to graze placidly on the short tundra grasses near the shoreline. They seemed very unafraid of me, so I figured that they had probably been transplanted here by the DOW (the Department of Wildlife), and they were somewhat used to being near people.

I will never forget the excellent surprise of getting to see so many beautiful wild animals in such an intimate setting, in such an unbelievable place.

After I'd eaten my lunch and downed a bunch of water, I hiked around the north end of the lake, edging slowly towards the mountain goats. I had my camera out again now, but for some reason the goats seemed skittish this time, and they started to climb back up the mountainside, away from me.

They were definitely not as relaxed today as they were yesterday, and I put my camera back in the pack without getting a single shot. I wondered why the difference? They had seemed very tame yesterday, coming up to me then as if they had been fed by hand.

After about an hour of resting at the upper lake, I decided I had better get on up to the summit of Eolus, as afternoon storms can build up quickly, even when the sky looks clear as a bell.

I have seen it go from totally azure blue—not a cloud in the sky—to all hell breaking loose in only twenty minutes—torrential rains, lightning hitting WAY too close, little streams turning into rivers in just minutes—that sort of thing. As I said, the high peaks block the view to far horizons, so it is hard to gauge the local weather with any accuracy.

Plus, I wanted to quickly get to the summit, and then back down to relative safety long before the sun started going down. I had about eight good hours to climb the remaining 1400 feet of mountain, take a few pictures and eat a snack on top after signing the register, then get back down, all the way down to where my tent and camp gear were, now already nearly two miles below me.

I gathered all of my loose gear, put it in the pack, did another idiot check, then hiked up the trail, watching carefully for loose rocks that might undermine my steps.

The trail, after leaving the upper Twin Lake, veers to the west, then up northwest into a tight, steep couloir—a tight chute between two peaks above—Peak Twelve and Mt. Eolus. At the top of the western limb of this couloir lies the summit ridge of Eolus.

But you can't access Mt. Eolus directly, going straight up the couloir—at least not without technical climbing gear, as there is a cliff at the top. You have to climb a few switchbacks up the couloir on the east, then straight up a steep creek bed to the top of a knife-edge ridge between Peak Twelve and Eolus. From there you then climb west to the Fourteener's summit.

Just before you get to the summit ridge, though, you have to cross a big, crazily tilted ramp—tilted the wrong way towards a thousand-foot drop if you should make any mistakes and slide off the edge. Not a pretty way to die.

When I was first looking up the steep trail in the couloir, I heard a strange grunting noise. I instantly turned, because the sound had come from down below me, down a steep embankment of rock, tundra, and dirt—beyond which the flank of the mountain extended down to the valley floor, which I could see fully 1500 feet below me. The embankment blocked my view behind me to the right, where the strange noise seemed to have originated, maybe a few hundred yards below me.

I suddenly and vividly remembered the weird sighting I had yesterday, and I instantly felt once more exposed and vulnerable. What did I think I was doing way the hell up here, anyway? I was now fearful and anxious, wanting just to go home all of a sudden. I hoped to myself that it was just one of the mountain goats, but I had my doubts. Do Rocky Mountain goats make grunting noises?

I now sat down on an outcrop of rock, and took off my pack to get out my monocular. I drank some more water while scanning the terrain below me with the glass.

"There! What was that?" I thought I saw something white move just below the lip of the embankment, just where it blocked the view. I looked carefully for a few moments, holding my breath. But the only thing moving was the tundra grasses and small white flowers in the breeze.

The grasses contrasted greenly with the remaining snow patches, most of which were melting off. I noticed that the breeze was now blowing more continuously, and gusting more than it had back at Twin Lakes.

I turned around and looked upslope—up the trail— to where I had a few minutes ago fully intended to go, before I heard the weird grunts. Now I wasn't so sure.

There was still a lot of snow up on the ridges and aretes above me, way up at the very tops of the rocks. Rivulets of white water flowed out of every possible melt path. Water even cascaded down the trail itself—up near the next ridge, anyway—and I wondered if it would be too saturated to walk on. It would also probably be really gusty and cold up there. I could see spray being blown off the rocks in occasional puffs, with misty rainbows forming briefly in the afternoon sun.

Just then, as if it had heard my thoughts, the wind blew violently down the couloir from the peaks above, blowing droplets of melted snow and sand at my face in a cold burst of fury. I cringed for a moment, turning my face away, and leaning instinctively into the slope to gain traction. The sand pelted my sunglasses, making little clicking noises.

"Damn! That was cold! Maybe I should just go back. This is insane!" I thought, realizing suddenly that I might just not have enough winter clothing with me to endure it up there on top, where the wind almost continuously blows. I had left my big winter parka back down at the tent.

I suddenly felt cold again, and a shiver went through me. I decided to at least walk to a better place, out of the wind, and put on some more clothing.

Although I was still on the trail, it was getting increasingly steep. Water was now flowing between my boots as I walked. They were now getting splattered with the brown mud. I looked above, where the trail looked like it went straight up a small drainage, and a little waterfall cascaded out where the trail should have crossed onto the ridge above. I hoped this was just a trick of the light, seen only from this odd angle, from about two hundred feet below.

I walked carefully on across the steep couloir, over to a group of boulders that rested on the southern flank of the mountain. Here, I would be more protected from the wind if it came roaring down again. I hunkered down between two big boulders, sitting on a gray piece of granite underneath.

I chugged some more water, catching my breath for a minute. I nervously looked back down towards the embankment, and I could now see a little ways further down it before the view was again blocked by the mountain's flank.

I should either push on and quickly make the summit—still about a thousand feet above me, according to the topo map, a stiff climb—or turn around here, going back down and opting for only two more nights of camping, one at my base camp below and one near the river, where I would have to wait for the train.

I was stuck in the Wilderness for at least three more days (including today) no matter what I did, so I decided I should go ahead and make the best of it. I would climb as long as conditions permitted.

I decided I would turn around and go home if the wind was howling too hard up on top of the ridge. Otherwise, I would go ahead and climb to the summit. I put on my fleece pullover, then my nylon rain jacket.

I warmed up quickly, and I realized that I might get too wet from sweating if I wasn't careful. I would have to strip off the fleece if that started happening, allowing the sweat to evaporate a little. (I hadn't yet heard of Goretex, a fabric that allows your sweat to evaporate while still keeping you warm).

I started plodding back up the steep, snowy, wet cou-loir. The trail was now composed of loose rocks and sandy brown mud, which caused me to slide down a little bit with every step—one step forward, two steps back. The zig-zags of the trail went steeply up a series of stair step ledges.

When I stopped and looked back down, it gave me ver-tigo, the couloir was so steep. I needed to be really cautious from now on, as one misstep could lead to disaster and maybe even death.

If I slipped off of even one of the big stair steps, I would possibly fall and tumble off of the lower steps for hun-dreds of feet before I would eventually come to a stop. This was not an option that I would survive, I realized. The wet ground and loose rock weren't helping, either. I grew in-creasingly anxious, all the while trying to keep myself calm.

My breathing was getting very labored now, due to the thin air at this altitude—about 13,000 feet above sea level. I was taking one step at a time, and then resting briefly be-fore making another one. Called the 'rest-step' by climbers, this method helps you not to outpace your oxygen supply. "Step up, breathe. Step up, breathe." I was still having a hard time getting a lung full of air, in spite of all of this.

I have climbed alone and I have climbed with others, and believe me—it is definitely harder climbing alone. You have no safety factor, nobody to bail you out of a tricky situation when you are alone. Plus, you are more prone to getting freaked out when you are alone, because there is no one there to reassure you, and your sense of machismo dwindles without someone there to impress. It often takes a lot more stamina and inner drive to force yourself to keep climbing, especially when conditions aren't at their optimum. It is just too easy to become another statistic.

I nervously decided to stop again for a minute, even though I wasn't at a very good place—right in the middle of a steep section of trail, with nothing to sit on.

I was still stupidly and obsessively wondering if the bone was OK. I took off my daypack and pulled it out of the bottom of the pack. I unrolled it gingerly from the now reddish t-shirt—the dirt on the bone had lots of iron in it, and it stained the white t-shirt a deep orange-red where the bone had touched it.

The bone was fine, and I carefully rolled it back up in the shirt again, stashing it once more securely down in the bottom of the pack with my camera, being careful not to drop anything out that would go bouncing down the precipitous slope below me. There was no way I could recover any of my gear should it get dropped now, and I potentially needed everything I had with me.

Cold shadows now suddenly enveloped me from above as I looked down the slope, shocking me when I realized what they were. I looked back up at the sky immediately above the summit block to my left and dark gray clouds were now skirting the jagged outline of the mountain.

The fog was torn into cottony wisps as the clouds scudded on the peaks, lingering like ghosts, strung along the interstices in the granite cliffs and rocky points. The temperature now suddenly dropped noticeably.

Another gust of icy cold wind coursed down from above, as if coming down from the clouds themselves—but it was really carrying them along. It was the downdraft of the wind front, and it whipped my hair around my sun-glasses, chilling me even more.

I stopped and dug out my wool cap, pulling it snugly over my ears, then re-shouldered the daypack. I slugged some more water, noticing that I had nearly drank a full gallon since I had left the tent early this morning. I still had a half-gallon in the pack, but that was probably just enough to get me back to camp, and not enough if I should have to spend the night up here for some reason.

But I could easily get water if I had to, as there were still thick drifts of snow in the perennial shadows under the cliffs, and the water was coursing out of them, then down into the depths below me. For now, I finished the gallon I was carrying, planning to fill it when I got to the little waterfall on the ridge above me.

After slipping one time too many, I finally untied my crampons from where they hung on my daypack, strapping them onto my boots and carefully tightening their leather straps.

Even though the trail was still too rocky for the crampons, I decided it was better to sacrifice some of the sharp points than to slip off of one of the ledges and get injured. There was still a lot of snow on them, making them slippery and perilous.

I also pulled my ice ax out of the straps that held it to the posterior of my pack, in case I started sliding. Ice axes are normally used on snow and ice, and it would probably only bounce off the rock if I ended up needing it. But maybe I could arrest a fall if I had to, in spite of the sections of bare rock all around and below me.

I finally made it to the little waterfall, and sure enough, it hadn't actually been pouring down the edge where the trail crossed to the high ridge above. I was relieved to find this out, as the trail was especially steep here, requiring the use of handholds as well as footholds. I clambered across the crux on all fours, and then sat next to the waterfall, where it cascaded precipitously down the mountain's face.

I filled my gallon jug about halfway with the icy cold water that burst off of the ledge, strapping it to the outside of my pack, where it would be handy to get at. I had to have both hands free to use the ice ax if I accidentally took a tumble.

The trail here continued on up the last section of the mountain's face, paralleling the jagged ridge that led to the summit of Mt. Eolus. Eolus was the Greek god of the wind, and we have such words as 'eolian', meaning 'wind-blown', coming from the same word root. This peak was aptly named, as the wind probably blows most of the time up here.

As if to mirror my thoughts, a cold blast of wind whistled through the jagged gaps in the ridge, and I actually had to lean backwards and hang on to keep from being blown off of the waterfall. The water in the little rivulet actually blew horizontally out across the chasm below for a few moments in the wind, countering gravity briefly before plummeting once again into the depths.

I suddenly once more felt like a total idiot, being up here in these conditions all alone. But here I was, and I might as well finish the fool's errand. I waited for the wind to die down a bit, then stood up tentatively, my crampons alternately scraping the rock and digging into the snow and mud.

A couple hundred yards further on, and I was on the top of the ridge, looking up across the big tilted rock ramp. I now had to sit down and take off the crampons, because I knew it was too rocky for me to get adequate purchase with them on.

Once I had tied them back onto the sides of my backpack, I carefully crossed the ramp, anxiously keeping as far away from the thousand-foot drop as I could. The clouds enveloped me, and for a few moments I couldn't even see where I was going. I was getting soaked with the fog, and I stopped yet again to put on my rain gear.

As I was fishing in my pack for my rain pants, one of the most beautiful sights I have ever seen abruptly stunned me, making me forget that I was in the middle of a potentially deadly ordeal.

The dark clouds to the northeast suddenly parted, revealing what could only be Jagged Mountain bathed in a bright yellow glow of afternoon sunshine, an incredible serrated row of gigantic golden glowing teeth, with the dark gray and white fog blanketing everything around it. In the foreground at my feet was the abyss, filled with gray and white clouds, wispy and surreal. If I jumped I would fall forever, it seemed. I had instantly lost all of my former fear at the realization of what I was seeing.

It was a fabulous moment of sublime beauty, and I will never forget it. I started to take off my wool gloves, in order to grab for my camera, but the wet clouds immediately closed in again, obscuring it all.

Just this one incident, lasting for only a few fleeting seconds, made the entire trip worthwhile. It was one of the most awesome moments of my life, and I only wish I could somehow convey the intense feeling of awe and beauty I had then to you. Moments like this are what make our lives meaningful.

I only vaguely remember the rest of the climb to the summit, as the scene I just described overshadowed everything else in my mind. After all these years, it is still etched into my vision. All else was just clouds and rain—footsteps upward in gray mud, my boots squishing, my socks soaked in spite of the waterproofing. It was a good thing I had wool socks on, as they retain much of their insulating qualities even when wet.

When I finally got to the top, the storm had come into its own, and I had only a few minutes to sit and rest, eat a few bites of gorp, drink some water, and sign the register (a capped, waterproof PVC tube containing a list of climbers' names used to ascertain the summiting of Fourteeners for documentation by the Colorado Mountain Club).

By the time I was finished, it was raining hard, and lightning was popping not too far away, dangerous conditions to be in on a high mountain peak. I was starting to shiver now, and I decided I didn't really want to die up here, so I stood up to go back down.

I had climbed down only about hundred yards when it started hailing, hailing hard. There was no place to hide, and the hailstones were very painful, like being pummeled by pea gravel. I had to get off of here, or I would die. Lightning struck even closer now, making me panic even more.

I was running now, or as near to running as one can be on a slippery, wet, muddy, and very steep trail, which was rapidly becoming obscured by the hailstones collecting in every nook and cranny. Lightning lit up the clouds for a brief second, and the immense sound immediately shook me to my foundations, like a mortar round on the battle-field, causing me to jump out of my skin.

"That was close—too close!"

I was freezing now, and I sensed that hypothermia wasn't too far away. I stumbled here and there, but I some-how made it back to where the ramp was. At least the hail had abated, for now. Now, it was only a freezing rain, al-most sleet.

I came around a big outcrop of rock, and there was the crazy stone ramp, all tilted the wrong direction, shrouded in fog, and now covered with slick hailstones and icy rain.

The clouds wisped tendrils up from the dark abyss, like ghostly fingers reaching up to grab me by my legs and pull me down.

I started warily across, but then stopped abruptly. I now had a sudden deep sense of doom, even more profound, actually, than the circumstances dictated. I suddenly felt like crying. Was I so spent that I was giving up?

But there was something more. Something moving from side to side on the other end of the stone ramp had caught my eye. I looked across the ramp intently, staring through the rain and fog at the shadows at the other end. Had I seen what I thought I had seen? The clouds suddenly en-veloped the scene once again, thwarting my efforts to see.

"There! There it was again—was that somebody standing over there?" The wispy tendrils were agonizing, frustrating me. "Who the hell would be up here in this crap—other than me, of course?"

Then the clouds parted, and there it was, clear as day—the Bigfoot! The Bigfoot was standing on the other end of the ramp, blocking my way! I couldn't believe my eyes! It was at least seven feet tall, and I realized it could crush me with just one blow.

It just stood there, looking stoically at me, staring directly into my soul, with no indication of any emotion. It was only about twenty yards away now. I could see every hair, every muscle, every minute detail of its face. Steam rose up from its flattened nostrils as it breathed into the humid air. It just stood there, looking over at me.

"Oh my God!" I thought. "This thing is going to kill me!"

But now I was strangely unafraid, and my thoughts contrasted sharply with my feelings. Then I did something that really didn't make any logical sense, in retrospect. It was so close, so tantalizingly close...now I could get a great photograph, and prove to the world what I had seen!

I slowly leaned the ice axe against a crag, and then I took off my backpack, watching the thing closely all the while. It just stood there and stared at me. I took off my gloves, one by one, the whole time watching the thing. I reached down into the pack, fishing for the camera, continuously looking directly at the creature. I refused to take my eyes off of it, as it could easily run up to me in only a second. Or, it could disappear behind the rock it was standing next to and be gone forever.

I now felt the coldness of the bone, wrapped in the now wet t-shirt down in the bottom of the backpack, and I realized now why the creature had followed me up here. The bone! Of course—it wanted the bone!

I felt deeper for the camera, and when I found it, I pulled it roughly out of the backpack. But the t-shirt had caught on the camera's strap, and it came tumbling out, landing on the wet rock of the tilted ramp. The bone came bouncing out, and it started towards the abyss, making a cracking noise. The two long apophyses broke off and flew out in pieces, little chunks plummeting down into the clouds, arcing down into the cloudy depths.

I immediately dropped the camera and jumped, scrambling to save the bone. Before it reached the edge, I caught it! But now I was sliding in the slushy hail headfirst towards the lip of the abyss—like a fool I had left my ice axe leaning against the stone, and I immediately knew I was now probably going to die. Just at the last second, I was able to turn myself, sliding sideways to my right, but my legs slipped over the edge, and I was going over, with the bone still firmly grasped in my left hand.

NINE: HANGING BY
A THREAD

I now suddenly remembered my father saying, so many years ago, "Stay here with the gear—I have to go see if I hit that deer. I'll be right back. Just don't go anywhere."

I had obeyed him, and I stood looking down the steep embankment he had carefully climbed down. It was only fifteen or twenty feet down, but that can seem like a lot to a ten-year-old child. It felt like I was on the brink of a big rocky cliff. My dad disappeared quietly into the oak brush down below me, running after the deer as fast as he could, without making too much noise.

The aspens around and above me had turned golden and red, and some of the leaves had already fallen, leaving a thin carpet on the grassy ground below. The autumn breeze had a sharp nip to it, and I shivered a little, in spite of the camouflage jacket and the black wool cap I wore. I suddenly felt scared, very alone, very isolated, very exposed, and very vulnerable.

The dark pine forest behind me sighed softly in the sudden breeze, and I had the sense that something was wrong, terribly wrong. A dark sense of foreboding enveloped me. Where was my dad? Why was he taking so long?

Then a horrible smell came to my nostrils, carried on the chilly wind coming from behind me. I turned slowly to see where it was coming from, and I suddenly saw the biggest, hairiest person I have ever seen, coming straight at me from the shadows in the pines. At least, I thought at first that it was a person.

But I realized immediately that this was no human person, and I instinctively backed away in terror. This was like nothing I had ever heard of, nor ever seen, and I knew I was now suddenly in danger of losing my life.

Without thinking, horrified, I backed right over the lip of the embankment, but I realized instantly what I had done, so instead of falling over backwards, I fell face first forwards, busting open my lip on the dirt (I had a scar on my lower lip for several years after that, but I couldn't remember where it had come from). Then I was sliding and bouncing over the edge, with dirt and rocks accompanying me.

I was able to grab a tree root right at the top, stopping my fall. But the creature was here now, and it reached quickly down to grab me. The fetid stench was now over-whelming, and it bared its teeth with a horrible grimace. Its black eyes somehow penetrated into my soul, and I felt a deep sense of sorrow.

Terrified, I let go of the tree root, and fell the rest of the way down the embankment backwards, hitting my head on a small rock at the bottom and blacking out.

The next thing I remembered was seeing the treetops in the autumn air, bouncing and swaying violently. My father was now carrying me, running in a panic back to the truck, breathing heavily, saying, "Oh God. Oh God. Please let him

live, please, oh God! Why did I leave him? Oh God, please!"
He bundled me into the passenger side of the truck,
wrapped me in a blanket, and we drove down the rutted
road, back to town, bouncing and careening crazily.

I spent three days in the hospital, and the doctor said I
had suffered a severe concussion. I was sick to my stomach
a lot, and I remember that the nurse wouldn't let me go to
sleep that first night, making me cry when she woke me.

I couldn't even remember what had happened to me,
and I couldn't answer their questions: "What made you
want to climb down that scarp? Why didn't you do as I
asked you and stay with the gear? What made you fall?"

The doctor had said I had post-traumatic amnesia, a
common occurrence when somebody hits their head hard
enough. I couldn't remember much of what had happened,
until now.

Now, I was hanging on to the lip of the stone ramp with
my right hand, holding the bone, clutched insanely in my
left. The drop beneath me was terrifying, a deep abyss filled
with menacing gray clouds and jagged, icy rock spires. The
cold rain spattered off of my raincoat's hood, and the droplets hit the back of my arm.

I noticed I now had a scrape just there, on the top of my
upper forearm, and the blood was just starting to ooze out
of it. My heart pounded in my chest, sounding like a freight
train roaring in my ears. Everything was now in slow motion, or so it seemed, somehow. Muddy rainwater ran off
the lip of the rock and poured into the neck of my raincoat,
soaking me.

I shook fitfully to my core, but I held on with all my strength. I could see the sinews of my right arm standing out under my wet, freezing skin. Why I didn't drop the bone, I can't imagine. I guess I was too freaked out on adrenaline to act logically. I just held on with one hand, a man obsessed.

The funny thing is, I focused intently on the rock. Not just on holding onto the rock, but the rock's qualities. It was wet, gritty, and slippery—I had gotten lucky and had grabbed it just where a little lip jutted up, giving me something to hold onto. But it was cold, so cold. I was just astounded at how cold the gray rock was—it blew me away for some reason.

My fingers looked like dead fish, they were so white and blue from the cold. The veins stood out on the back of my gloveless hand. I was glad now that I had removed my gloves, because they would be too slick to hold on to the wet rock.

My fingers were scraped and hurting, and I could just see where little mini-rivulets of blood were making the rainwater streaming down the rock red, just a little. I was seeing things in slow motion, close-up and personal. But I was oddly calm, like I was just observing, not involved somehow.

But then a horrible smell assaulted my nostrils, and I looked up to see the Bigfoot quickly approaching me. It was going to get me now, and I knew I was going to die. It probably wanted to make certain I couldn't return home with the bone, to prove its existence up here. I turned my head away, looking down in anguish into the clouds beneath me.

But I didn't want to fall—I was even more terrified of falling—so I just instinctively held on as best I could, my fingers slipping slightly on the wet rock, my grip failing. I was going to die—I was going to die either way. I looked back up, back at the monster.

The Bigfoot was now swiftly kneeling down, and the nasty smell was starting to make me retch—it was that close to me. It had a grimace on its face, just like the one I had seen when I was ten, but it also had a soft expression about its eyes, one of deep concern, a look of compassion and empathy. I could see every hair on its head, in vivid detail.

I thought of just letting go, like I had done before, when I was ten. But I wasn't going to have to, as my grip finally failed, my fingers skidding roughly across what remained of my handhold, and I started to fall. I was suddenly in free-fall, looking down now into the murky depths, and it was the most horrifying moment of my life, but it was also the most serene. I was only in a movie, and I was seeing it from afar. It was all over now.

But just then, the Bigfoot reached out and grabbed me by the right forearm, in a tight, enormously strong grip. Its huge hand easily enclosed my entire upper forearm and elbow, leaving bruises on it later. The creature swiftly pulled me up back onto the ramp, slightly dislocating my shoulder—I felt a sharp pain arc up into my neck and down into my upper back.

As it did so, I suddenly had the courage to look up, up into its eyes. They were black as night, and I felt the hackles go up on my neck. That look—that look. It was the same look I had seen in the eyes of the other creature so long ago, when we were out hunting, when my father was still alive. It was a look of extreme concern and caring, of almost human warmth and understanding—not a look of rage or offended pride. Tears welled up, and the image went blurry.

Then I was suddenly lying there, face down on the cold wet granite, shaking with fear and hypothermia, with the bone still tightly clutched in my left hand somehow, now draped down at my side. I was face down, looking at the muddy rivulets streaming under me, going into the depths where I was only moments ago nearly doomed to plunge.

I wondered if the creature would now insist on me handing the bone over, and I tentatively looked up again, my bleeding, aching right arm now stretched out in front of me on the ramp.

I raised my head, arching my sore neck backwards to look up at the creature, and the hair on my arms and neck suddenly stood up again. But it wasn't from fear—I was already now feeling the full effects of the fear, and there was no way it could get any worse.

I was in the electrical field, a strange sensation that is like a sudden rush of startling energy, making you instantly and keenly aware of your short mortality. The electricity gives you a rush like adrenaline, but sensed in every pore of your body, rising up in every hair on your head.

I had been in the electrical field of lightning only once before, a few miles to the northwest from here, up on the top of Engineer Mountain—that was insane, too, and my friends and I had had to run for our lives as lightning popped all around us, like spears flung from the hands of angry gods.

Now, as I looked up from my prone position on the wet rock, up at the beast, a bolt of lightning struck the pinnacle just behind it, the flash outlining every feature, silhouetting the black creature with an explosion of white and yellow fire, making its hair stand on end all over its body—it was that close!

BOOM! The report shook us both instantly, with no delay between the flash and the explosion. I could see little streamers of electricity swarming down the face of the rock. A thump shook my body, and I could hear small pieces of shattered rock flying all around us in the rain, clattering over the lip of the abyss. My ears kept ringing for three days afterward, traumatized by the enormity of the noise.

Terrified, the Bigfoot now ran swiftly, disappearing around the rock outcrop at the other end of the stone ramp with a dexterity that would shame a mountain goat. My eyes had streamers of white fire on their retinas that only faded after a few seconds, but I could still see around me in spite of this. My benefactor was gone, just like that, before I even had a chance to say "Thank you." I started laughing hysterically at the thought.

I finally collected my self and stood up shakily. I was feeling around, kneading my shoulder, when I brushed the pocket of my shirt, and I was immediately stricken by another paroxysm of laughter. The M80 in my pocket—I had totally forgotten it was there!

TEN: INTO THE CAVE

But I didn't laugh for long, before the laughter turned into tears—tears of shock, tears of relief, tears of fear, tears of anguish, tears of joy. I was feeling so many emotions at once, my mind was so overloaded, it made me think I had suddenly gone insane.

It was still raining, and another lightning bolt nearby made me jump neurotically. I was on the verge of losing it completely, but I had to force myself to get up onto my feet and start across the now terrifying, slick wet ramp. I shook like a jackhammer, and my legs were nearly useless.

I stopped for a minute and packed the bone back into the bottom of the daypack, wrapping it into the reddened t-shirt again. I also noticed my camera, on the wet rock, there where I had dropped it. I put it inside the pack also— I really didn't think I would be taking any more pictures up here. It had gotten scraped a bit when it hit the rock, but other than that it seemed none the worse for wear.

I crab-crawled up to the far side of the granite ramp, using both my arms and legs, and then pulled myself up by the crags and rocks on the safe side, making myself stand up shakily. It took me a while to edge myself across, but

I felt a strong sense of triumph when I finally made it to where the creature had disappeared around the outcrop.

I was still shaking to my core with shock and trepidation, but also with the freezing cold and hypothermia I was now feeling. I looked nervously around the far end of the outcrop, but I couldn't see anything through the wispy fog. Lightning crackled just down the ridge from me, and I felt the electricity in the air again.

I was now just as afraid of freezing to death up here— or being struck by lightning—as I was of the creature, so I decided I had to continue on, on down what looked like the trail—now just a muddy rivulet streaming with slush and rainwater down the middle of the summit ridge, all wrapped in mist and rain.

I felt inordinately elated when I randomly came upon a cairn in the rain and fog (a cairn is a crude stack of rocks that merciful souls put along the trail for others to tell which way to go). I silently thanked whoever had built it, feeling that they might have just saved my life.

I had had my life saved twice within a half-hour. The whole ordeal was starting to get to me again, and I began sobbing once more, standing there and leaning on the cairn. But I sternly forced myself to stop. I had to move on.

I had to get the hell off of here, or it wouldn't matter whether the creature had saved me or not. Being an emotional wreck wasn't going to help me to survive. My shoulder now ached, throbbing with every move, and my arm was still bleeding, making the sleeve of my rain jacket stick to it.

But I was still alive, in spite of all that had happened.

This thought calmed me considerably, and I soon made it back to where the little waterfall cascaded over the lip—so I was encouraged even more, now realizing that I was still on the trail. I had been moving enough to warm up a little, although I was still going through fits of uncontrollable shivering, a sure sign of near-hypothermic conditions.

"I just have to get the two miles back to the tent, where I can get dry and get some hot tea in me," I thought. I stopped in spite of the rain—I was still drenched anyway—and I forced myself to eat some trail mix and drink some more water. I reached down into the backpack yet again, feeling for the bone.

Even though I was still dazed, dizzy from the ordeal and suffering from the freezing cold, I made myself fill up my water jug at the waterfall, in case something else happened and I was forced to bivouac for the night—even though I actually figured that a night out up here in my condition wouldn't be survivable.

It would soon get too damned cold and wet, and the chances of living through it without sufficient clothing or a sleeping bag would be slim.

When I climbed down over the lip of the summit ridge, I realized that I was now unbalanced, with the full jug in one hand, and my ice axe in the other. I decided that the ice axe wasn't going to be of any use on all of this bare rock, so I stopped again and strapped it to my pack.

Clouds now filled my vision, nothing but clouds, and I often even lost sight of the trail, stepping cautiously into what might have been nothingness had I not been down off of the cliffs where it wasn't quite as steep. This slowed my progress considerably, as I had to be sure of my footing or I might fall again.

Freezing cold bursts of wind battered me, making me stagger crazily, as if I were drunk. I now had no idea where I was, as all of the landmarks were totally obscured by the storm, and the trail could be anywhere.

I was definitely lost, so I stopped once again to fish out the topo map from my backpack's top pocket.

I was sitting on a big boulder—that was all I was sure of. I dug out my compass and tried to reconnoiter. I knew I had to continue to the southeast, but without any visible landmarks, I had no way to orient myself in the mist.

I should have been close to Twin Lakes by now, but there was no indication that I was near them. Everything was completely enshrouded in fog now, and the daylight seemed to be waning. My watch said it was already 5:25. I had been stumbling around for over three hours, and I hadn't yet found the lakes where they should have been.

I was lost, and the thought was deeply troubling to me. This had only happened to me once before, and that time I had been spelunking in a cave. I had been underground, after all, so I gave myself a pass on that one.

Now, I might as well have been underground for all I could tell of the landscape around me.

My right arm was still bleeding through my rain jacket sleeve, and I was feeling weak. I knew I would have to stop somewhere and attend to it—at least find some sort of shelter where I could take off the rain jacket and see how bad it was.

My shoulder still throbbed, but it seemed to have abated somewhat. That, or I was starting to lose all sensation due to the cold. I was shivering all of the time now, not just at random intervals. I had read about hypothermia in mountaineering medicine books, and all of the symptoms fit.

I was sluggish and clumsy, and I was concerned that I would do something totally stupid. My self-confidence was waning with every minute spent out in this horrid storm. I was frustrated and angry for allowing this to happen.

Just then as I was musing, another big gust of wind came up and tore the damn topo map right out of my hands. It flew away into the mist like a big white bird, and I immediately lost sight of it in the clouds. I now had no way to figure out where I was, but I didn't really care anymore. I couldn't find my way even with the damned thing, anyway.

I got up from my seat on the boulder and started to stumble along again. I fell a couple of times, just catching myself in time to avoid tumbling precipitously down the steep slope.

Then I stepped on a loose piece of granite at the wrong angle, twisting my left ankle hard. Not only was I freezing and lost, but now I was limping. After a few more steps, I sat down and sobbed for a few minutes. My ankle hurt when I tried to rotate my foot around, and I was sure I had sprained it.

I leaned back and shook my fist at the sky, screaming curses at the top of my lungs. I was losing my mind now, and it was only a matter of time until I would be completely finished.

"Who cares anyway? Nobody would even give a damn!" I thought cynically.

I got up again, and limped roughly, each step more painful than the previous. The loose rocks and muddy rivulets of water were just there to taunt me further, I imagined.

I had no idea how far I had come, no idea how to get back to camp, and no idea if I was even going to make it. I continued in this state for what seemed like hours, but was probably only a few minutes—my sense of time was all fouled up as well.

I finally sat down one last time, determined that I would just stop here and die. I was just so cold, shivering down deep in my core, and I knew I would be gone soon. I had read that the end game of hypothermia really isn't that bad, as you just stop shivering and might even feel warm, just before going to sleep forever. That's what I was going to do—I was just going to lie down and go to sleep.

I leaned back to get more comfortable, expecting to find the slope at my back. Instead, I roughly fell over backwards. For a second I thought I was falling, but I immediately hit the ground behind me with a thud.

"What the hell?" I thought.

There was suddenly no slope behind me like I expected, and for the first time in hours I was abruptly out of the rain. I was now looking up at the lip of a big boulder that had rainwater running off of it in sheets, pouring down onto my rain pants, spattering loudly.

I pulled myself back up and looked around, craning my sore neck to see where I was. Behind me was darkness and jagged rocks sloping up into a damp cave.

The big shelter cave! I had somehow stumbled onto the shelter cave I had seen from far below, and I breathed a sigh of relief at the realization. I might just be able to get dry in there, and I quickly stood up, staggering and groping my way into the darkness.

It was definitely drier in here, but it was so cold and humid I could now see my breath in the backlight. I immediately took off the rain jacket and got out of my wet sweater and long john underwear. My right arm was a mess, blood all down it from the top of the elbow to my wrist. I had to peel the sticky clothes off of it, and I wondered how I had scraped the top so severely. It must have happened while I was slipping over the edge of the chasm where the creature had saved me, as I had rolled over onto my side.

I pulled the t-shirt from my pack, with the bone still in it, shivering uncontrollably the whole time. I carefully unwrapped the bone, setting it gingerly on a flat rock and putting the t-shirt on, the red soil stain on the shirt transferring to my wet hands and chest. Even though the t-shirt had gotten damp when it hit the rock, it was still drier than the long johns. I warmed a little after a while, and it was the first time since I had been on the summit ridge.

It was now that I finally realized that I had left my gloves way up above, on the stone ramp where I had encountered the Bigfoot. My hands were icy and unresponsive, hard to use, and I probably already had some frostbite.

"Damn it! How could I be so stupid?" I berated myself. I hadn't noticed the gloves when I picked up the camera, and I figured they must have blown away.

Even so, I was still able to get into the shirt, and I put the sweater back on after wringing as much water out of it as I could, painfully. I would have to medicate my scraped arm at some point, but first I had to get warm—if I had a chance. I still had the fleece tied to my pack, although it was dripping wet. I wrung it out as well, my hands hurting like I had arthritis—but I kept squeezing.

After I pulled the fleece on, I warmed up enough for the shivering to subside a little bit. I reached into my pack and made myself eat several handfuls of trail mix, and then drank a bunch of water. I had to have metabolic energy to get my body temperature back up. After a few more minutes, I felt a little warmer still. The shivering was gradually going away, now that I was inside where I could get dry.

I might just make it, after all. Even though I could still see my breath.

But I still had to get down to camp—somehow. I stood up again and limped stiffly back to the cave's entrance. Wispy clouds filled my vision, with gray rock and occasional green tundra being revealed here and there where they parted. I could only see a few yards in any direction, and it was still raining, although it seemed like a little less than before.

But now I was shocked by another harsh realization. The darkness inside the cave was quickly being matched by the waning light of the setting sun above the gray clouds all around me. I had no way to find my camp so far below me, especially after dark. I was going to have to stay here and try to weather it out. A bivouac in the cave was not my first choice, but it had now become the only one.

If I could only light a fire, I would be OK. But there wasn't any fuel so far up above the tree line, and my spirits sank again. It was going to be a cold night, and I might just freeze to death—not a bright prospect.

I got the little emergency flashlight I carried in my survival kit out, shining it around the inside of the shelter cave. I hadn't noticed it before, but my nostrils were now assailed by a horrid stench—the same horrid stench I had noticed when the Bigfoot had grabbed me.

This place was apparently one of its lairs, and the thought was in no way comforting. I only hoped it wouldn't decide to come in here, in spite of the fact that it had rescued me. I sincerely hoped it had disappeared down valley, far away from me.

I shone the flashlight up above, in a corner of the cave where two of the giant boulders met at an angle. There might be a flat spot up there where I could possibly lay down and try to get warm. I grabbed my pack and climbed up to it. Sure enough, there was a place there that was flatter than the rugged rocky floor of the rest of the cave.

As soon as I got up to it, I noticed something else that was weird. There was a big pile of dried grass and twigs up in there, bunched up into a big ball with a flat place in the middle, like some kind of nest. I would now be able to make a fire—there was plenty of dry kindling!

But I stopped myself, after thinking it through for a minute. I could make a fire, but I could also use some of the grass for insulation to try to stay warm.

I stuffed some of the nasty, smelly grass into my rain jacket after putting it back on again. I probably looked ridiculous, like the Straw Man in the Wizard of Oz, but I didn't care. The thought made me laugh a little, and the humor of it made me forget my dire circumstances for a few seconds.

Soon, I was warming up nicely. The shivering had nearly completely stopped, I realized with relief. I gathered more of the grass off to the side to build a fire, where it wouldn't light the rest of the nest pile on fire. I pulled out my Zippo from my pants pocket, but the wick was wet, and it wouldn't light no matter how hard I tried.

Fortunately, I keep a fire-starter in my survival kit, and I dug it out. (Fire-starter is a piece of metallic magnesium that you strike with a flint rod to create sparks.) Although I'd never had to use it to survive before, I'd practiced with it a little when I'd first bought it, just to get the hang of how it worked.

I bunched some of the dry grass together around the magnesium, and then drew the flint roughly across it. It sparked brightly, lighting up the walls of the shelter cave for a second. After about ten or twelve tries, the dry grass finally caught. I blew gently on it, and I was able to feed a few small twigs from the nest into it, creating a small fire.

I had a fire—a real fire! I was elated now, and I knew I might be able to survive.

ELEVEN: FIRE

I carefully fed the little fire twigs and grass, warming my hands by cupping them close to it. This hurt, and my hands throbbed—a sure indication that I had at least some frostbite. I was careful not to warm them too quickly, as I had heard that this is what causes the most damage in cases of frostbite. My hands became a little easier to use now. I hoped I hadn't damaged them too much.

My dampened spirits were lifted at the sight of the merry little fire. Its light reddened the cave walls, flickering and dancing. The grass burned quickly and the few twigs that were there wouldn't last too long, so I was very cautious to keep the fire low, just enough to keep it from smoldering out.

Its warmth was palpable, and I scooted as close to it as I dared, trying to get myself warmer. The little plume of smoke wafted up towards a hole where the rocks met, a thin tendril of gray rising in the increasing gloom.

I decided to build up the fire a bit so I would have time to dress my wounds. I keep a first-aid kit in my daypack, and this was actually the first time I had ever used it, in spite of how many times I had been out camping.

I once more peeled the rain jacket off, and the insulating grass fell out on the ground. Some of it stuck to my upper arm where the blood had dried. I held the flashlight up and inspected the wound closely, brushing off the grass.

Although it had bled quite a bit, it had now finally started to clot, and I realized that the best I could do was to simply put on some anti-biotic ointment and then wrap a couple of big pieces of gauze on it. I did so, and I taped them securely on with white medical tape. I saved the paper wrappers the gauze had been in, in case I needed them to light another fire.

It would get really cold up here tonight, I realized, and if I let the fire go out I might not get another one lit. But if I was careful not to let this happen, or to burn up all of my fuel, I could probably keep myself warm enough to make it to sunrise.

I put all of my clothes back on, and then re-stuffed the insulating grass back into my raincoat. I had already gotten a little chilled, so I returned to the fire and warmed myself.

Sunrise. Sunrise was a long ways off, I knew. I leaned over a bit to check the watch that hung from the lanyard on my pack's zipper. It was only 7:30 in the evening now. But two hours had already passed somehow since I had last checked, and I was grateful for it. Now, if only the rest of the night would go by as swiftly.

I took a minute away from the fire to climb up into the grassy nest, testing it for comfort. The smell was overpowering, and I gagged, nearly puking. This was not going to be any picnic, but I was still thankful that the nest was here. I could get over the odor if I was tired enough, I realized.

It must have taken the creature a long time to haul all of this plant material up here, as there was a quite a bunch of it. The tundra outside definitely wasn't long enough to build a big nest like this, so all of this longer grass had to have come from the valley below.

As I said, though—the grass burned really fast, and I had to jump up from the nest immediately to go feed the fire before it went out.

"This is going be a long weary night of nothing but fire-tending," I thought. "Oh well—it's better than freezing, that's for sure!"

I ate a few more bites of trail mix, and then decided it would be best to conserve the rest for later, when I might really need it. I had a tin of sardines with me as well, so I figured I might just have enough food to get back down to my camp, where I had more stashed in the tent.

Then I remembered that I had neglected to hoist my big backpack up into a tree to keep my food away from bears. I only hoped that no bears would tamper with it—or anything else, for that matter—as it was my only hope for making it all of the way back down the seven miles to the railroad. I didn't think I could make it without any food left.

But I still had to get through the night before I would have to worry about what was left for me down below. If I managed to survive, I would find out in the morning.

I sat and fed the fire for what seemed like forever, and I had finally gotten completely warmed up once more. I was nearly dry now, with only my boots and socks still wet, along with the bottoms of my pant legs. It was a good thing I had brought the wool sweater and the wool fleece, as wool will actually keep you warm even when it is wet. I guess it has enough natural air space in it to do so.

Eventually I grew extremely weary, and I knew I would have to resign myself to crawling into the smelly nest to get some much-needed sleep. I would just have to let the fire go out, but I knew I could probably get another one going, as I had carefully dried out the wick on my Zippo, and it was now lighting just fine.

I was bone-tired, and the thought was ridiculous to me. "Bone-tired!" I chuckled at myself for being so foolish about the bone. What if it was just some elk or moose vertebra, and not a Bigfoot bone at all? Had the Bigfoot actually followed me up Mt. Eolus to get it back? If so, why didn't it just grab it out of my hand up on the rock ramp when it had the chance to do so?

Even so, I obsessively checked on the bone again. It was now down in the bottom of the daypack, this time without any wrapping. I had broken it when it fell on the ramp, anyway, so I was now less careful with it. Besides, I was beginning to think that maybe it wasn't as important as I had made it out to be. Who really knows?

Nevertheless, when I crawled up into the big grassy nest, I dragged the daypack with the bone in it up with me—just in case.

I curled up around the daypack into the fetal position, as I had already started to get chilly, being now away from the fire. Although I was now warm, the temperature in the cave was dropping dramatically. But it really didn't matter—I was too tired to care.

I pulled the reeking grass and twigs around me, trying to cover up against the cold. I finally managed to get somewhat comfortable, and I fell into a deep sleep.

TWELVE: RESCUE

I was in a beautiful green valley now, and I felt so peaceful and serene. This was what Eden must have felt like, so relaxing and joyful. I knew I had my loved ones close by, and I knew that they were safe, happy, and well fed. The valley below me was verdant and healthy—the trees and meadows were so green, and the river sparkled down there, in the yellow sunlight.

The warm yellow sun above felt good, and I sat down on a big boulder to luxuriate in it. We were all up here, in our mountain home, and I knew that just over the hill from me, others were there, just like us—living in peace with their surroundings and enjoying every moment of their productive lives.

But now suddenly I felt as if something had gone wrong. A cloud had suddenly gone over the sun, making the landscape go dark somehow, all at once. The air was now getting chilly. Night was approaching.

I called out to my mate, but she didn't answer. I called out to my children, but I now sadly sensed somehow that they had gone away a long time ago, never to be seen again. I wanted to weep. I sobbed for them, and the echoes of my voice died out finally, in the shadows of the trees.

Even the trees were different. They were more spindly, drier, sick looking. Strands of sere gray-green moss hung from their branches, like the hair of an old woman.

I felt a strange sorrow overwhelm me. It occurred to me now that I was the last one, the last of my kind to wander the Earth. The sky had now turned a sickly yellow-brown, and I realized I was abruptly in the midst of the big forest fire I had 'dreamed' of before—or only thought I had—except now it was just below me, down the hill a bit in the trees. I was in the middle of the woods, with no possible way to escape but to go up the mountain, away from it.

This was the real fire now, and it was coming rapidly up the hill towards me.

Then I heard dogs barking at me from down below, their low voices startling me, and I knew I had to run, to run away through the smoke as fast as I could. The Others were after me now, and I knew I wouldn't survive their savage, predatory bloodlust.

I ran—I ran so fast I could see the trees blur with motion as I passed by them. But it was no use—the Others kept coming up into the heights, swarming. They were coming from all directions—all around me in the plains that now stretched out below.

I clutched the bone tightly in my now older, leathery hand. The bone's sharp points were dulled, rounded by long handling. It had yellowed with age.

I soon managed to sprint up a small conical hill. When I got to the top, I was able to see out all around me—the smoke from the fire hadn't reached up here yet. The smoke of the Great Burning was still far below me.

I was now in the middle of a vast plain, up high, and the fire was spread out all around, burning the vast landscape below me. Big mountains rose on the far horizon, blue sentinels, witnesses to the cataclysm.

There were the Others as far as I could see all around down below, extending into black, spotted masses spread out to the horizon, and the forest fire had now become the fires of their torches.

They all had torches and pitchforks, maces and knives. They were all pushing, jostling against one another to get at me, a giant swarm coming up the hill to kill me.

There were now millions and millions of them climbing up all sides of the hill swiftly towards me, and I knew then that I had I only a few seconds before they would overwhelm me. They were now big black army ants with jagged weapons of steel to pierce me through, and torches of red fire to burn me.

The smoke was acrid, burning my nostrils now, rising up from all around, from the vast burning plains below. The sky rained down cinders and red-hot ashes, blinding me with gritty tears. The black army was suddenly on me now, and I lifted up my head in a dreadful howl of anguish and pain.

"Hello? Hello, is anyone in there?" The sound echoed slightly off the back walls of the cave.

I awoke to a voice, the first human voice I had heard in over three days. It was daylight outside now, and I had somehow slept through the night without waking up once. The weird dream now faded swiftly, and I lifted up my head to look over at the cave opening. I immediately noticed that I was now shivering again.

BRAD MORRIS

"Hello? Maybe you imagined it, honey." The voice was now talking in quieter tones to someone else outside the mouth of the cave. "C'mon, hon, let's get on down off of here."

"No! No, no, no! Please don't go—don't leave me up here, please!" I yelled out, but my voice was surprisingly weak and scratchy. "Please help me!"

"Hello? Is somebody in there?" The voice was a man's, and I could sense the concern in it.

"Please, please don't leave me here!" I cried out weakly. "I don't want to die here—please!" I was overwhelmed once more with emotion, and I broke down, sobbing. The thought of being abandoned was excruciating.

"Where are you? I don't see you." the man called out.

"I'm up—in here—in the back—of the cave." I rasped out between sobs.

"OK, OK, just hang on, we're coming! Come over here, honey. You were right—there's somebody in there!"

I pushed myself up by my elbow, and then fell back down into the smelly nest. I was shocked at how weak I was. I hadn't realized until now how much the ordeal had taken out of me. I felt like I was going to get sick. I was all jittery and weak, and I felt feverish. This was the last thing I needed right now.

A man in hiking shorts with a staff now clambered into the mouth of the cave, and I could see his form silhouetted against the outer daylight streaming in. I have never seen a more awesome sight before or since. I was saved! I sobbed again at the thought of it, and I laid back into the stench of the grassy nest, too drained to move.

112

"Hey! Hey, Buddy! Are you alright?" The man was shining a small flashlight now into the cave, and the light blinded me for a second when I looked directly into it as I lifted myself up again.

"I am now!" I said. "You have no idea what I've been through!" My breath caught again with the emotion, and I shuddered, a house nearly broken.

"Hey, it's OK. You're amongst friends, now. We'll get you out of here." Behind the man a second silhouette came into the mouth of the shelter cave, and I could see that it was a woman.

"I'm Jerry Struthers, and this is my wife Cecilia. She thought she heard someone cry out up here. I guess that would be you, right?" He had clambered up to where I was, and he held out his hand to shake mine.

"Yeah, that would be me. I'm Brad Morris, and I can't tell you how nice it is to meet you!" These were the first words I had uttered since I'd left the train three days ago. It seemed like years.

I'd been in a nightmare, but I was now abruptly awake, and the sun was streaming into the cave's triangular opening.

I sat there while Cecilia wrapped my ankle tightly with a bandage, along with a couple of tent stakes that made it into a handy splint. They fed me some beef jerky and heated some tea using their little alcohol stove. This revived me greatly, and I asked what time it was. My watch was hanging from my pack—too far to reach.

"Let's see, it's 10:32 Tuesday morning," said Jerry. I had slept long after the sun had risen in the valley below. I was stiff and weak, but I was feeling a little better now.

They were wonderful people. They saved my life. They helped me down out of the cave, down the now brightly sunlit, steep talus slope. I slid and nearly fell several times, and without their help I might have injured myself even worse than just a sprained ankle and some road-rash from the ordeal up above.

I think my main ailments were mild hypothermia, dehydration, weakness, and hunger. They got me to where my camp still stood, the tent covered in dirt and sagging a little, but nothing else amiss.

I still keep in touch with them, writing them letters once in awhile. We get together once in a blue moon and have a few beers, but they live nearly 400 miles from me, so we don't see each other that much, though we went up to the Tetons a couple of years ago. But I digress.

They stayed with me for an additional night while I rallied further, generously making certain I was feeling strong enough to make it to the train the next day. They even had to completely change their itinerary for me, as they had planned to go up over the Hazel Lake Trail cutoff to camp above timberline at Columbine Lake, and then climb Jupiter Peak the next day.

But since they decided they were going to stay with me, they would be one day short on their trip, and they would have to just climb Windom and Sunlight Peaks, and then get back to the train on Saturday.

But they insisted that they stay with me, and I was extremely grateful for it. I must have looked wretched.

The rest of that afternoon they fed me the all of the beef jerky they had in their daypacks and made me hot tea and hot Jello, helping me feel like I was actually alive again.

Then, after making sure I was all right, they hiked back down valley, to where the shortcut to Hazel Lake Trail split from the Chicago Basin trail.

They had set up their camp there last night in the storm, and had been on an morning reconnaissance hike up towards the Fourteeners when they found me. I kind of thought I might not see them again, but only because I am cynical, and not because of anything they had done or said.

But to my surprise, in a few hours they came trudging back up to where I was, this time with their full big backpacks on. I had crawled into my sleeping bag and slept, still exhausted.

They checked on me, then proceeded to set up their camp again. I got up out of my tent and had some more hot tea.

I felt a little ashamed that they had to go to so much trouble for me, but Jerry only said, "Aww—forget it! We figure you'd do the same for us!" Cecilia voiced her agreement.

"Yeah, we don't want to hear you mention it again!" she said.

"Just get back up on your feet as a way to repay us, OK?" and she smiled at me. They had some freeze-dried beef stew, and they made us all a sumptuous meal.

Anyway, the next morning, after I had slept ten more dreamless hours, they once again made me a hot meal (oatmeal with dried fruit), and then after making sure I was fine with hiking out alone, they bade me goodbye and hiked on up towards the Windom Peak and Sunlight Peak trail. I watched them go, and I had the warm feeling that I now had new friends for life.

The hike down the valley to the train was a little shaky in places, and I had to rest a lot, but that suited me just fine, as the weather was now spectacular (it figured). I still hobbled some on my sore ankle, but Jerry and Cecilia's ministrations had helped immensely, and the fact that I was now carrying less food and only a gallon and a half of water made my load much lighter than it had been before.

I still ended up having to set up camp down at the Animas River again, because I didn't arrive there until after the afternoon train had already departed. At about two o'clock I first heard it coming—the engineer blew the whistle upriver from me, so I knew that this was the last train from Silverton to Durango today—but I was still way up above, about two miles from Needleton, where the train stops.

I did my best to hurry as fast as I could, still limping but limping faster now. But it was no use. The evening train usually stopped for a few minutes just to let off a few backpackers, instead of making an extended stop there. I was still over a half mile up the trail, huffing and hobbling, when I heard the train's whistle again. They were leaving, I knew, and I heard the chuffing of the locomotive as they clanked on up the river, gaining speed.

The last few cars of the train were just going around the last bend out of Needleton when I got to the valley floor, where I could finally see them through the trees. Maddening, but it was what I now had to deal with.

So I had to set up camp again, and I won't bore you with all of the details. I was a little slow at it, but I got some more dinner in me after awhile, and I knew I was going to be OK, finally.

The next morning, I had to have some help getting my backpack up on the train—I was still that weak. The conductor actually put the big pack into the storage car for me, then came back over and pulled me up onto the passenger car.

After a few minutes of waiting to go, a short older bald fellow in striped shorts said, "Excuse me—I can't help but notice how you look like you've been to Hell and back."

"Yeah, you could say that" I replied. "I feel like I've been dancing with the Devil."

THIRTEEN: HOME

I was able to get my heavy pack off the train and onto the ground when we finally arrived in Durango, not needing any help this time, as gravity was on my side.

I was also able to get the thing into my little Toyota's trunk, after walking through the station and across the parking lot. My first mission here in Durango was to get a motel, a shower, a good hot meal, and then a six-pack of beer. This was exactly what I did, and the luxury of it all was unbelievable! You really must try pampering yourself, especially just after you've almost died.

For the first time I realized that I really had a reason to celebrate. I had celebrated for many reasons in the past, but now I really had a good reason. My life had been spared—not once, but twice! I was ecstatic.

The long drive home the next day was just that—a long drive. When I finally arrived in Boulder, I went straight home, unloaded all of my stuff, took another shower, and settled in for a nice relaxing few days before I had to go back to work.

I was still a little weary, but I was on the mend.

Of course, I hadn't yet had the time for it all to process in my mind, and I didn't yet realized that, in spite of the whole episode having a cathartic effect for me, it would also end up giving me PTSD—that's what a psychiatrist diagnosed me with some years later, anyway.

I ended up having nightmares about the Bigfoot for years, in spite of the fact that it had actually saved my life. The weird dreams persist to this day, although they are fewer and farther between, and they don't have the emotional impact on me that they used to have.

You have to be careful which people you tell certain things, as many are put off by strange talk of silver beasts that stalk backpackers in the wilderness. I think they are afraid of finding out what this might mean—that we aren't alone here on Earth, like we have always imagined that we were. We aren't the only intelligent hominid here—I know it.

I took the bone to my friend who was studying paleontology at Colorado University in Boulder at the time, and I asked him to find out what kind of an animal it came from, without saying anything about what I thought it might be.

When he gave it back about a week later, he said that the professor he had given it to had examined it carefully. He had even gone into the archives to compare it with other bones, in addition to getting the opinion of one of his peers, before making the judgment that it was a bear.

Most likely an old sow black bear—it was exceptionally large—that had probably died on the upper edge of the gully where I had found it, and then gradually gotten buried, subsequently creeping with the soil down the hillside and mixing into it. It did look like it was really old, but without expensive carbon dating there was no way to really know how old it was.

It was difficult to be sure what the bone was, because the "wings" (my friend informed me that the correct term was "transverse processes") had been broken off on the face of Mt. Eolus, and fallen into the foggy abyss up there. Of course, nobody knew that but myself, and I kept it secret.

I still don't know what the bone was. Was it a Bigfoot? Maybe not, at least according to those who should know. But then, why was the big silver-maned creature stalking me up the mountain? I guess I will never know the real answer.

The bone got lost in the shuffle, over the years. I thought I had it in a safe place, but I moved around a lot. I got married and divorced twice, and even lost the contents of a storage shed once when the rent didn't get paid by my now ex-wife. I think maybe the bone had been in there. Whoever bought it at the auction had no idea what they had purchased, I mused.

It really doesn't matter, though. I don't think I would want it to be known if the bone really had been a Bigfoot's—even though it might mean fame and fortune for me. It would just attract millions of more people out into the wilderness, which is already getting degraded enough. And I didn't want to betray my benefactor.

Recently, I was up at Chautauqua Park outside of Boulder again, though I now live in a little town on the Western Slope of Colorado.

It was another glorious summer night. I could see out across the prairie again, and the magnificent sight brought rushing back to me the memory of that night so long ago, when I'd been up here just after the ordeal.

I realized keenly that I am now a changed man—actually not the same person at all, except perhaps in name and general appearance. I now have the years attached to me, and they oftentimes weigh me down. I am not so spry anymore, not like I was then.

I long for that time, that time so long ago. If I could only somehow relive it, even the horrible trauma of it all. Just to feel young again would be miraculous.

I never made it back up into Chicago Basin, but I was at Needleton once, when I took my daughter and my grandchildren to ride the train from Durango to Silverton and back. We got out for lunch there, and I took them up the trial to Chicago Basin for about a half mile. My grand kids are seven and five years old, and they were born to hike, I am proud to announce.

Then we had to get back, before the train left for Silverton. The engineer blew the first whistle, telling everyone to get back to the train. The echoes lasted forever, and I felt the presence of the harsh, high, awesome granite peaks, just there, just above all these trees. We got back on the train, and I made sure everyone was wearing their sun goggles, to keep the soot out of their eyes.

That was a great day.

I climbed a few more mountains in the 90s—a couple more Fourteeners, and a few Thirteeners—but I had a daughter by then, and I figured it was time to settle down and make a living for her sake. My vacations became fewer, and they became less and less strenuous as time wore on.

I still get out as often as I can, but I'm not climbing Fourteeners anymore. Too much work, at my age.

I often think of "Silver"—that's what I call the Bigfoot. I had to name it, to identify it, to categorize it, to somehow secure it in a place in my mind. It was too wild for me to comprehend, otherwise.

I wondered if it had lived to an old age, or maybe it was even now still alive? Had anybody else ever seen it? Was it alone? Did it have enough food up there, where the land is so harsh and unforgiving?

Whatever it had been, I owe my life to it. I think of it with fearful respect, and I know my soul has grown because of it. I look at the whole world with different eyes.

I guess being stalked was really a blessing in disguise.

About The Author

Brad Morris is a 68 year old retired schoolteacher and ex-computer programmer. He enjoys helping others less fortunate, so he does volunteer carpentry for a local community outreach program for those in need. He loves the thought of being able to assist others.

Brad enjoys the outdoors greatly and makes sure his daughter and grandchildren enjoy it also. They recently climbed Mt. Garfield outside of Grand Junction, Colorado—it was his fifth time—and he says he won't ever do it again (he has said this every time). It's just way too steep for his rickety old knees. So, he says he will just stay on the easy trails, admiring the exploits of the youngsters from afar.

www.ingramcontent.com/pod-product-compliance
Lightning Source LLC
Chambersburg PA
CBHW070707290526
45790CB00001B/479